Ladder or Lottery

Ladder or Lottery

ECONOMIC PROMISES AND THE REALITY
OF WHO GETS AHEAD

Gary A. Hoover

UNIVERSITY OF CALIFORNIA PRESS

University of California Press
Oakland, California

Library of Congress Cataloging-in-Publication Data

Names: Hoover, Gary Allen, author
Title: Ladder or lottery : economic promises and the reality of who gets
   ahead / Gary A. Hoover.
Description: Oakland, California : University of California Press, [2026] |
   Includes bibliographical references and index.
Identifiers: LCCN 2025027246 (print) | LCCN 2025027247 (ebook) |
   ISBN 9780520402621 cloth | ISBN 9780520402638 ebook
Subjects: LCSH: Income distribution | Social contract—Economic
   aspects
Classification: LCC HC79.I5 .H66 2026 (print) | LCC HC79.I5 (ebook) |
   DDC 339.2—dc23/eng/20250918
LC record available at https://lccn.loc.gov/2025027246
LC ebook record available at https://lccn.loc.gov/2025027247

GPSR Authorized Representative: Easy Access System Europe,
Mustamäe tee 50, 10621 Tallinn, Estonia, gpsr.requests@easproject.com

34   33   32   31   30   29   28   27   26   25
10   9   8   7   6   5   4   3   2   1

Contents

Illustrations

TABLE

Preface

This book is a conversation I have had over many years with individuals from the political left and the political right. With those very high up the income ladder and those barely holding on at the bottom. With those who claim to have our economic system totally figured out and those who have no idea what is happening around them. It is a conversation about how so many people can look at the same situation and draw vastly different conclusions about what they are seeing. The real difference appears to be their perspective.

Perspective seems to matter greatly in the context of where one feels they are and should be along the economic and social spectrum. While some feel the sorting out of positions along this spectrum has a very clear merit component, manifested by industry, sacrifice, and dedication, others view the final ordering as being much more opaque, where requested actions, once taken, do not seem to align with expected outcomes. I refer to the actions and the resulting outcomes as being a *social contract* between society as a whole and the individuals who make it up.

While some see the system of assigning relative positions in the social and economic context as working well, or as well as can be expected, others find inconsistencies and flaws of a major and minor order in the process and wonder why their individual actions did not lead to desired outcomes, while those same actions did work for some of their peers. From the perspective of some, the final sorting might seem more like a lottery or much more of an endeavor of risk than one of assured upward mobility. And if there is some level of randomness present in the final ordering, can we really ascribe choice or blame to how things ended up for some?

I have endeavored in this book to look at the same situation through the lens of many individuals who have thought about this question of economic and social mobility and what it actually takes to move up. The book pays particular attention to a group who feel they have done all that society has asked of them, through the social contract, but argue that the final ordering has not fairly situated them, given their actions. They feel they are undeserving of their lower station in life. This group sometimes gathers in protest to make it clear to all they have not failed the social contract, but rather the social contract has failed them. They want it known that while some of their peers might not have tried and could be considered deserving of their fate, these individuals are uniquely different and undeserving, given their actions.

Through many conversations with scholars from around the world, I have endeavored to reconcile the true differences between how society might view individuals and their actions and how those same individuals see themselves and what they have come to expect from the tasks they have accomplished.

From my earlier studies on poverty and income inequality to my later works on domestic and transnational terrorism to my investigations of differences in economic opportunity, this book is the culmination of my discovery concerning unfulfilled expectations from the perspective of those both looking in and looking out at the same set of circumstances.

I would like to thank and acknowledge the support of the Murphy Institute at Tulane University, for without their support, this book could never have been written. My staff are to be commended for dealing with me as I toiled on this book while attending to my duties as executive director. It was also because of the interdisciplinary nature of the Murphy Institute that I was able to interact with scholars from fields as varied as law and business to those in philosophy, engineering, and the health sciences. Those interactions have enriched and informed my thinking in ways that have allowed me to look beneath the surface of some very pressing issues.

I cannot forget to thank my many colleagues from several universities, think tanks, and private-sector institutions who challenged me to address issues about the nature and purpose of a lottery when an individual is prohibited from buying or unable to buy a ticket. I have been pushed not just to investigate where our current system lies but also how we got here. I was asked to leave my lofty perch in an ivory tower and write a book that would be understandable to a vast array of people. I am glad I was able to add some perspective on where we can make inroads toward making our social contract function better in the future.

I would also like to acknowledge an individual at UC Press who added invaluable assistance, gentle guidance, and clear objectives along the way. Michelle Lipinski must be commended for her dedication to seeing that this work was accessible to a wide range of readers while never sacrificing scholarly rigor.

1 Who Are the Haves and Have Nots?

The easiest way to start this book is with an explanation of what prompted me to write it in the first place. Like any scientist, I noticed a phenomenon happening around the globe, specifically, that we have a great deal of wealth and income disparity, especially here in the United States. I then did what most scientists do and made a hypothesis about how and why this phenomenon was occurring. Afterward, I set out to see if there were testable examples that would prove or disprove what I had speculated about. After spending half my career doing research and looking at the data, the conclusion I have drawn is that humans are not lacking in mercy or charity toward other humans who have less. Rather, it seems that something has led many in the world to believe that having less is a matter of choice, and as such, those who have less are simply exercising their free will and should not be interfered with. I thought that something, maybe nature or just bad luck, caused divergent starting points and paths for various cohorts of peoples. In essence, something put some people on the path to become members of the "haves" group and something else put others on the path to become members of the "have nots" group.

With these two groups identified, I wondered if their paths ever crossed, and if so, what mechanism caused it. Some would argue that there is a pathology or cultural barrier that inhibits those on the lower rungs of the economic and social ladder from ever rising above their circumstances. Think of the common story of fleas kept in a jar. After making countless attempts to leap out of the container, which were met with bumping their heads on the lid, the fleas learned to jump just below the barrier but no farther. The story goes that even after the lid was removed, the fleas, which had become conditioned to jump only so far, never realized that all they needed do was jump higher to get out of the container and escape. Per this logic, what was holding back the "have not" group was their own minds and conditioning, for in truth, all they had to do was jump higher.

Maybe this line of reasoning could hold for some at the bottom of the economic and social ladder, but it could not explain how billions of people on the planet find themselves on the outs in terms of material resources. It occurred to me that the answer might exist in the way I posed the question at the start, for I used the term *economic and social ladder*. If we imagine a ladder, we see that the path was laid out for those on the lower rungs. All they needed to do was climb! By random luck of the draw, some individuals might find themselves starting on the lower rungs of the ladder, but they certainly did not need to stay there. They just had to climb. One foot. One hand. One step. They too could have and share positions higher on the economic and social ladder.

Pushing this ladder analogy even further, I speculated that those at the top of the ladder did not need to be overly concerned about those below, since all they needed to do was climb. As mentioned before, maybe those down at the bottom of the ladder like it there. Maybe they suffer from a pathology, like the fleas, that does not allow them to go higher. Regardless, the rungs are there. Those at the top see them. The question is, why do those at the bottom not see them?

I could imagine those at the top of the ladder stating that the ladder could be even higher were they not constrained by providing funds for the development and maintenance of the ladder for those at the bottom. They could claim righteous resentment toward those at the bottom who did not appreciate or understand the magnitude of their largesse.

I also noticed that there seemed to be a substantial number of people at the bottom who believed in the ladder and also agreed that simply climbing was necessary to reach the top. However, some found themselves disillusioned and frustrated after having tried to climb but getting no higher, or at least not as high as they felt their efforts should have taken them. Sure, they were lower on the ladder, but they did not deserve to be in that position because they had sincerely tried. Some of these individuals would state that they had tried on several fronts and on several occasions to climb. They were not conditioned fleas; they were true believers in the rungs of the economic and social ladder. They wanted it known that they might be on a lower rung, but unlike their nonclimbing and deserving peers, they were different. They wanted the world and especially those at the higher rungs to realize that something was not right with the ladder and that it was not them. How else could it be explained that all their efforts had resulted in little or no upward movement? Maybe the ladder was missing a necessary rung, or a rung was damaged? Maybe the rungs had been placed too far apart? Or maybe too many individuals already occupied the rung above and there was no more room? They wondered if the ladder had been greased by the traffic of those who had gone ahead of them and now the rungs were so slippery that no amount of effort would be enough for them to be able to hold on.

In the end, these individuals might feel that, instead of a ladder, the more appropriate analogy might be a lottery. How does a lottery work? Everyone does the same thing, namely, purchase a ticket. Of course, not all tickets bought will be winners. In fact, most will not win. How are those who made the effort and bought tickets but did not win to be distinguished from those who never bought tickets? There is no publicity for losing lottery participants. Only the winners are noted and celebrated. The key difference when buying a lottery ticket is that the purchaser knows there is an inherent risk involved and no certainty of success. This idea of cost, or risk, belies the point made earlier about people being at lower rungs of the economic and social ladder by their own doing. They could have simply been one of the unfortunate people who did not win.

So, when enough of these undeserving souls found themselves in the same regrettable situation, trying but getting no higher, they formed a group to protest. They wanted two things made clear. One, they had tried, so there was something wrong with the outcome and not the input of their efforts if this was truly a ladder. And two, they were distinguishably different from their peers, even if they all happened to share the same rung on the economic and social ladder.

After setting this up as my premise, or hypothesis, for this book, I set out to find examples of social contracts and how they were supposed to work and how many of them actually worked. In other words, did rungs on the ladder exist and function properly? I wanted to establish what a social contract was beyond saying that it is a ladder with people occupying rungs. That will come in the rest of this chapter. Some chapters of this book look at case studies of individuals who formed groups to protest the promised outcome of the required action, namely, climbing the ladder. I also wanted to lay out how these groups arrived at the conclusion that they were undeserving of their position on the ladder and whether the broader society agreed with them. Maybe there was a misunderstanding of what action should have been taken. Maybe the groups wanted too much for too little effort. Or maybe, just maybe, the social contract had failed them and not the other way around.

The term *social contract* needs a bit more defining than what I have described to this point. To put it simply, doing prescribed actions will lead to prescribed rewards. That is what I am calling a social contract between a society and its citizens. To be clear, the term is not new nor is it specific to a certain academic discipline. Probably the most commonly thought of form of social contracts comes from philosophy. Individuals in a functioning society learn to cooperate for their mutual benefit and form a government to that end. That government will protect the rights of the citizenry and help ensure order. Many tomes have been written by the likes of Thomas Hobbes, John Locke, Jean-Jacques Rousseau, and Immanuel Kant, among countless others. The questions that arise out of these thought experiments are ones about what rights must be ceded to government and how that government will ensure a fair and just distribution of resources. Will there be some form of progressive taxation or other social programs that will be distributive in nature? Many questions arise when thinking about this form of a social contract and countless authors have attempted to answer them.

Another way of thinking about the term *social contract* comes from law. In this context, the term may differ a bit from how philosophers use it, but fundamentally there is a legal theory around the relationship between a citizen and the government. There have been numerous books written by legal scholars that explore what power the government has and how laws passed by government are to be thought of. For the sake of security, what rights should or could citizens be willing to give up? What if the government passed a law that stated no citizen had any right to privacy? For the sake of domestic security, a social contract could implicitly include that there would be no privacy granted regarding a citizen's person or property that could impede the government from eradicating any form of national security threat. These threats could be ones that have not even happened yet, and an individual's intention to disturb the peace could be enough to invite scrutiny by the government. This is not to say that such a contract exists or even should exist, but only that it could. These are the serious issues that any society must grapple with. One way to leave all these legal ponderings behind is to simply have no society. Everyone would be an individual who only looked out for their own best interests, without regard for others. In essence, we could simply take the "social" out of society.

There are many ways that this concept of the social contract could be explored, from work done by sociologists to the field of literature and fiction, to international relations and even education. The books written about how these various fields address this issue fill up many sections of local libraries. All of them are interesting in themselves and worthy of future exploration. For the sake of this book and how I have come to observe the world, this concept could be boiled down to one word or phrase, and a poor distillation of it would be the word *promises*. By acting collectively and agreeing to given societal norms or governing practices, individuals are able to have better and fuller lives than they would otherwise. Of course, this word doesn't capture all the nuances in a given field of study, but it can give readers a common starting point for what I am conveying.

The field of economic study was not mentioned earlier. It was saved for last, given my particular academic interests and the use of the term in the title of this book. Many economists would say that the social contract relates to the relationship between groups, such as laborers and business owners, over economic rights and responsibilities. For instance, what exactly is a business owner buying when a wage or salary has been paid to a worker? Can an owner stipulate that, given the fact that they paid a wage, the worker should not be entitled to things such as paid leave or rest breaks or even overtime pay?

That is not, however, the only context in which the social contract arises in economic discussions. An alternative discussion is probably most closely related to what is to follow in this book. That is, what is the role of government regarding the distribution and redistribution of resources that is fair and equitable for all citizens? These ideas might be most closely tied to philosopher John Rawls and the "veil of ignorance," in which individuals agree to principles around economic justice without knowing their rung on the economic ladder. But moreover, what is the role of government, if any, when knowing one's rung on the ladder actually leads to discouragement? For example, let's consider my definition of the undeserving. Should the government be responsible for correcting aggrievement caused by displeasure with being lower on the economic and social ladder?

In a research paper published in 2016, I and fellow economist Erik Kimbrough ran a laboratory experiment with college students to gauge how much social comparison matters in investment decisions.[1] In essence, the experiment involved individuals who were different in terms of their wealth and income. Some were high wealth/income individuals, while others were not. Under the veil of ignorance, no participant knew the status of the others. They did not know the income or wealth status of anyone but themselves. They were all given a task to perform that had the potential to increase their future payouts. Not surprisingly, when there were no social comparisons, the participation rate among high and low wealth/income individuals was statistically the same in performing the task that led to higher payouts. However, once individuals were able to see their status on the economic ladder as compared to the status of their peers, despite the fact that nothing else changed and their potential to increase their future payouts stayed the same, there was a dramatic decrease in participation by low-income individuals. We wrote, "In a simple life-cycle consumption and investment task, we find evidence that social comparison increases the rate of suboptimal investment choices among the income-poor. We argue that this is driven by a discouragement effect on those who are less likely to benefit from their investments—despite the fact that investment by all types leads to the same increase in expected utility."[2]

It could be argued that these low-income individuals in our experiment had just as much chance as their peers to take advantage of these investment opportunities, and since they did not participate, they must have wanted to be where they were. They were somehow deserving of their lower-income status since they did not engage in the investment decision at the same rate as their higher-income peers. The experiment was designed such that no one would ever lose anything in a real sense, so it was suboptimal not to engage. In essence, the experimental design was the social contract, and by not participating in the investment decision, those individuals ceded any expectation of sympathy. To be clear, the experiment was not about the social contract, or deserving and undeserving, since I had not formulated the ideas for this book at that time, but the outcomes of the experiment have informed my thinking. Since I was acting as the government or society in this experiment, was it my role to point out those individuals' failings?

At this point, I should clearly introduce a few terms to help us distinguish between the two groups of individuals who find themselves at the lower end of the income distribution or otherwise on the outside looking in at society. There are those individuals who tried to fulfill the social contract but have experienced a failure that is not of their own doing. In other words, they followed a socially acceptable road map to success but did not receive the expected benefits that they felt were due to them. These individuals will be termed the *undeserving*. They felt that they should have been higher up on the economic and social ladder, given that they engaged in the actions that they were assured would lead to upward mobility. In fact, their rallying cry might be *I do not deserve to be here!*

On the other side will be individuals who are also at the lower end of the income distribution or otherwise on the outside looking in at society. But, as stated earlier, they have not engaged in the action required by the social contract, and those higher up have determined that they must somehow be deserving of their lower station in life. After all, with the creation of a perfect, or at a minimum, a perceived perfect road map to prosperity, their lower social status must be a choice—a choice that these individuals picked for themselves. These individuals are deemed by society to be the *deserving*. In essence, they got what they deserved for not following the plan.

There have been many excellent books written about charity and giving to the poor or less fortunate dating back to biblical times. With regard to charity, there are two ways to approach the problem of poverty, even if society believes that some individuals are where they are due to no fault of their own and others are there due to their own inaction. One method could provide some form of charity through giving and material help directly to the unfortunate. Maybe an agency could be created to handle the distribution of goods paid for through a tax of some form. A second idea could be simply to eliminate poverty by creating a system where there are no real poor, only those choosing a lower station in life. There is a quote about giving a man a fish and he eats today, but teach him how to fish and he eats for a lifetime. It has been ascribed to several cultures and philosophies, but the idea remains that giving to the poor becomes unnecessary because there theoretically should be no poor or less fortunate. In this way, anyone claiming poverty need only be pointed toward the social contract, which assures upward mobility for all if the path is followed. Neighbors helping neighbors would be an outdated mode of thinking. The charity would be that instead of material sustenance being provided to someone claiming to be in need, that person would be encouraged to fully engage with the social contract. In other words, give a person a ladder and they can climb up themselves.

One other benefit of this social contract, as I have defined it, is that it could eliminate guilt. Those citizens with plenty would not need to feel obligated to feel pity for the less fortunate around them or feel the need to give them help. After all, help was provided in the form of a plan that would allow them to enjoy the same benefits as others on a higher rung of the economic and social ladder. It would allow people of greater means to make the statement, "I got here by my own efforts and others can do the same." This is a point that will be discussed in greater detail in the next chapter. However, the key term here is *effort*. If effort truly assures mobility, then the statement becomes more salient.

I use the terms *deserving* and *undeserving* in a context totally different from how they have been used before. Per Michael Katz's excellent book *The Undeserving Poor: America's Enduring Confrontation with Poverty*, the terms I use here would make no sense. Most readers who have even casually explored the issues of poverty and inequality in the United States will also be perplexed by the use of my terms. So, there will need to be some adjustments.[3] The reader should be cautioned to take a moment to let the new use of old terms take root. The undeserving are deemed by society to be those who tried to climb, or in other words followed the social contract, but have lower status. The deserving are those who did not try to climb or follow the social contract.

To some extent, this book and Katz's are not all that different. He explains the "irony of optimism" in that he states that others believed "with scarcity off the table, individual failings marked persons as all the more undeserving in a world of possibility where poverty no longer was inescapable."[4] In essence, he articulated what I believe many people in society believe, that in the ultimate system of commerce and industry, anyone who is born poor certainly does not have to stay that way unless they chose to, either through laziness or some moral failing, which makes them somehow deficient. In my book, it is the social contract that is the ultimate system. A person might be born into poverty or simply be lower on the income ladder than where they want to be, but certainly they are not bound to stay there if they simply engage in the actions prescribed by the social contract. If they do not engage in society-endorsed actions, then they have gotten what they deserve and are accurately situated on the income and societal spectrum.

There will be little room for sympathy for any lower-station person, whether we label them undeserving or deserving. However, the undeserving, as I have defined them, will do more than look for sympathy from those above, given their plight. They will, in some instances, state clearly that they took proactive steps to correct their situation and still find themselves unsatisfied with their station in life. In the middle chapters of this book, I will present several case studies of groups of individuals who believe they are undeserving of their status.

The obvious drawback of the social contract, as it has been laid out here, is something Katz brings into focus: What about those unable to engage in the activities required by the social contract? He writes of widows, children, and those who should not be held responsible for their status. Are they to be categorized as part of the deserving outsiders, meaning that they have chosen to be where they are? The easy answer, which comes from the social contract, is that once they have been deemed faultless, their local community or smaller community of family, some of whom would have gained benefit from the social contract, can fill the void. In the next chapter, I will discuss statistics on poverty and inequality, and those numbers are usually given at the family or household level; thus, there is someone for whom the social contract directly worked. In other words, they are responsible for those unable to engage in the required actions of the social contract themselves. My observation is that society spends little time drawing such fine distinctions between lower-rung categories. This book will show that any type of lower-rung status is frowned upon, but that the undeserving poor will have more to say about their situation.

Not all those on the lower rungs of society's ladder will go quietly into the night. There is strength in numbers, and as we will see, when a critical mass of the undeserving gather with others who find fault with the system, there can be some form of political, economic, or social protest. What I argue is that what matters much more than the numbers of poor and suffering is the composition of that group. By composition, I mean the percentage of undeserving people who find themselves on the lower rungs of the economic and social ladder. If that percentage reaches a critical mass, protest will follow. It is easy enough to turn a blind eye to a group of individuals with whom one rarely interacts. However, it is harder when that group refuses to be ignored and wants to distinguish themselves from their deserving counterparts, and also has reason to believe that their complaints are legitimate, maybe even righteous. The key for them is to show that their circumstances are no fault of their own actions, even though society might not want to draw those distinctions.

The undeserving might call on the business world as an example, since commerce and industry are the drivers of the modern economic juggernaut that has led to such prosperity around the globe. In my 2023 presidential address to the Southern Economic Association, I made the point that if society thinks of poor people as being where they are due to their own negligence or lack of use of the social contract, then this might be considered a form of user error.[5] After all, the system is there and perfectly designed to lift up anyone who applies themselves to engaging in the actions required by the social contract. Improper use can be viewed as a bad user interface. However, in any other business context, when nearly 15% of operators could not properly use the system or product, there would be an immediate demand for a recall or, at a minimum, a product redesign. Whether the product is something like faulty software in a word processing package or children's toys with parts missing, it really does not matter. Even if the product is not posing a threat to the health or safety of the individual, 15% failure would mean that there should be some reevaluation.

Typically, these redesigns are not as important to the material well-being of nearly 15% of the citizenry of a country. Yet, when it comes to poverty and suffering, society is quite comfortable with the idea that some are deserving of their plight, and their complaints of a faulty user manual should not be seriously considered. It would be interesting, if not quite sad, to hear that 20% of children choking on small parts of a poorly designed toy were deserving of their fate, as opposed to creating an age warning or redesigning the toy. To say that the toy is perfect and the fault lies with the children could be true, but a rethinking of the product is still required. In the case of the social contract, once a critical mass of the undeserving form, they will demand that the system work as intended or be redesigned. The key difference here is that these individuals believe in the value of the system; their complaint is about the execution of the plan or system. Whereas others might call for the wholesale dismantling of a system seen as fundamentally unfair, these undeserving people only want to call for the system to work for them as they have seen it work, or believe it worked, for others. In fact, they might be more zealous in their defense of the system than those who actually have benefited from it. This is a point that will be brought to light in Chapter 5, particularly.

Some have argued that racial discrimination, which was absolute law during slavery and then supported legally by many states during a sustained period of Jim Crow laws in the South, is a social contract. The case being stressed is that the results of acts of discrimination have left cohorts of racial minorities undeservedly poor, or outsiders. Per the terms I used earlier in this chapter referring to a lottery, the claim could be made that these individuals were never allowed to purchase a ticket and could not enter the broader discussion. The argument, on the surface, seems to fit with what has been laid out here.

Economists note that wealth is "sticky" in that it is generational and transferable to future generations, whereas income is less transitory. Keep in mind that annual income minus expenses becomes savings, which when accumulated over years becomes wealth. This distinction is important in giving individuals resources to further their education or engage in entrepreneurial activities. This point will be very important in both Chapter 3 and Chapter 7.

One of the paradoxes of the social contract, as I have laid it out, is that there needs to be some type of definitive action taken by the person. It is that person, who can point to said action, who will feel they are undeserving of their position on the economic or social ladder if the benefit received does not meet expectations, given the action taken. Even though some action(s) is (are) required, there could still be the need for resources to achieve the goal, for instance, start-up capital to begin a business or tuition to go to college.

With regard to wealth, two statistics immediately jump to mind: mean wealth, or average wealth, between families; and median wealth, where the median is the wealth level that splits the population in half. In 2019, the mean wealth of white families in the United

States was nearly seven times as high as that of black families. More so, median wealth between the two groups stood at nearly eight times higher for white families.[6] Where there is clearly defined action called for by a social contract that requires an initial outlay of resources, such action would be more difficult for families with less wealth. Because wealth is sticky and transferable, present and future generations are at a disadvantage if their wealth is lower.

Cutting edge research done by Derenoncourt et al. shows that, historically, the gap between white and black wealth was as high as 55 to 1 in 1860, and was 6 to 1 in 2020. That ratio of 6 to 1 has remained relatively stable for many decades.[7]

It is more than simply the fact that there has been a historical gap in wealth between the two groups. It is that one of the main vehicles to gaining wealth, that is, income, is vastly different. The two groups occupy different strata on the income scale. From Figure 1, the reader can see that black households were overrepresented at the bottom of the scale. If the reader will indulge me for some statistics, the point can be made clear. The mode of a distribution is the number that appears most often. It is identified by the top, or crest, of the hills in the diagram. It is clear to see that the top of the hill for black incomes occurs at approximately $19,000, while the same mode point happens somewhere around $33,000 for white incomes. This particular distinction is important given that in 2016 the official poverty threshold for a family of three in the United States was $19,105. What Figure 1 shows is that black households were over-represented at the bottom of the scale and underrepresented at income levels over $40,000.

If we look at net worth, which is accumulated assets minus out-standing debts, we find that black households with college educated individuals in 2018 had a median net worth of approximately $70,000. Note that a white household with individuals with less than a high school education had a median net worth of nearly $83,000.[8] The black householder could legitimately make the claim that the social contract has failed them and they are a member of the

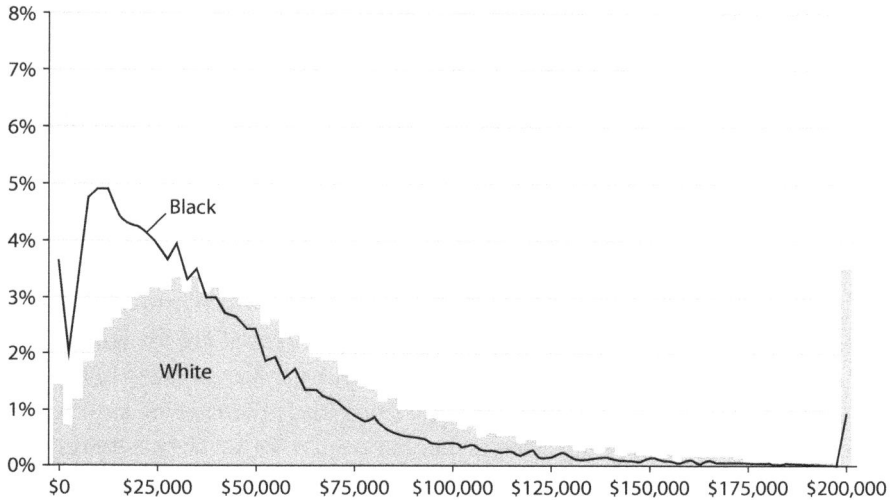

Figure 1. Shares of white and black Americans with a given level of income, 2016. *Source:* Kochhar and Cilluffo, *Income Inequality in the U.S. Is Rising Most Rapidly Among Asians*, citing Pew Research Center analysis of the 2016 American Community Survey (IPUMS).

undeserving. After all, they did receive an advanced degree and yet find themselves lower on the economic ladder than those who did not take advantage of the free and compulsory education provided by society.

Further to the argument of net worth comparisons, the most valuable asset owned by most individuals is their home. Homeownership is seen as a cornerstone of American society. It is critical to building stable communities and fostering a sense of belonging among neighbors. There is an argument to be made that even homeownership, which is key to retaining and transferring wealth, is disparate among races. In 2022, the homeownership rate among black people was slightly over 45%, while the rate for white people was over 71%.[9] This type of difference could lend credence to the idea of a racial divide among those included in the undeserving. In Chapter 8, I will add more "meat to the bones" of homeownership and the social contract.

Despite all this evidence, and much more that I could have presented, the idea of racial disparities and discrimination does not fit the definition of the social contract as I have defined it. The reason is that I defined the undeserving as those who took an action that was not properly rewarded. If being born into a certain race bestows the benefit or makes one deserving of their status, then no action was taken. Simply put, people do not choose to be born into a given race group. However, I need to be careful not to conflate the source of the grievance. If a black citizen states that he or she engaged in the action required by the social contract but finds themselves among the undeserving, the question becomes one of whether they were the victim of bias based on their race or whether there was a failure in the social contract, or some combination of both.

In the case of the combination option, where there was a mixture of racial discrimination and definite action taken by the individual, there must be a careful parsing, which is not clear nor easy. For example, say a black individual lives in an underprivileged neighborhood. The illegal practice of redlining, where individuals in a given neighborhood are denied access to credit markets or services in a discriminatory manner because of their race or ethnicity, leads to lower property values in the area. Since schools are primarily funded by local property taxes, these neighborhoods offer a lower standard of education. An individual in this neighborhood takes full advantage of the schooling available to her, yet she still finds herself unable to be competitive on the job market due to the education she received. The argument, as has been laid out previously, would be that she should feel undeserving of her station due to the action she took, namely, getting all the schooling she could, which then should have assured her upward mobility, given the social contract. However, if the root cause of her protest is racial or ethnic discrimination from the redlining, then although she has legitimate reason to complain, she would not fit in exactly with those protesting only due to violations of the social contract. The actions and the discrimination have been mixed, and it would be difficult to figure out where one stopped and the other started.

Suppose she did take action as prescribed by the contract by seeking to be an entrepreneur or attaining more education; if she were denied economic mobility due to her race, then there is no action she could have taken because her race is not an actionable item. The defining feature of the social contract is the action taken and the positive results promised. If society stipulated in the social contract that all individuals of a given race—say, black individuals—were not entitled to the benefits of the social contract, which was clearly the case during slavery in the United States, then all white individuals could protest violations of that social contract if they did not benefit more than the most prosperous black individual. Under that system, neither race would need to do anything except be born. That is not the type of social contract that I am envisioning in this book.

In my imagining of the social contract, anyone can be considered aggrieved by violations of the social contract without the associated presumption of a pathology placed on an entire race or ethnicity, which normally accompanies most racist beliefs. In other words, not all individuals of any race are fleas, as from my earlier example. This pathology idea manifests itself in ascribing to the culture of a particular race or ethnicity the belief that they are deserving of their station on the economic and social ladder due to an inability to perform the tasks required of the social contract. Having not engaged in said tasks, the group as a whole should not be expected to be anywhere other than among the deserving lower-rung individuals. As I stated, no group of individuals connected by race or ethnicity behaves in a uniform manner, and there will be a spectrum of thoughts and actions.

To be clear, I am not making the argument that racism is not worthy of protest. Nor am I claiming that racism or other discriminatory acts have not left people at levels of disadvantage as compared to other groups. The problem with discriminatory behavior, as a social contract, is that it requires no action. The race or ethnicity of the individual has been prejudged, and as such, blanket assessments of ability or cognition are assigned. With an action-based social contract, such as the one described earlier, anyone of any race can feel they are undeserving of their station on the economic ladder because of a failure of the contract to act as promised, given their actions.

What I hope that readers will take away from this book is that society needs to think seriously about all the aspects of a social contract. Issues about access and benefit will be key. There must also be care taken in deciding which activities to promote as society enhancing. The mechanism of dispersion and efficiency of benefits will arise as issues. I will provide examples of what activities are included in the social contract. Until now, I have been particularly vague in articulating what these actions would be so that the reader might have time to form their own thoughts before we dive in. Even though actions are supposed to be open to all, there should be some examination as to whether the distributional aspects of the activities matter. In other words, is it possible that some citizens never had the opportunity to engage in those activities, and should they be considered as deserving or undeserving of their station in life?

The book then takes a turn, in Chapters 4 through 7, and focuses on those who consider themselves undeserving. One question that arises is whether society, as a whole, agrees with their assessment. What happens when there is a critical mass or a tipping point of these people who see themselves as being undeserving of their place in the economic and social order? Finally, given the definition of the social contract and those left out of it, the book will make some predictions on where we might see the next tipping point growing and how that might manifest itself in society. These protests cannot be good for a well-functioning society and economy, so we should put some effort into thinking of ways to diminish their likelihood.

2 Poverty and Inequality by the Numbers

This chapter expands on the provocative statement I made in the previous chapter: The US and the rest of the world have a rather remarkable tolerance for high poverty levels. If we see poverty or being lower on the economic ladder as a choice, then there really is nothing that can or should be done to help such people. The social contract has already been devised as a system to lift up anyone from any level on the social spectrum. There is really no need for despair given that those below can simply embrace the activities of the social contract to lift themselves out of poverty or change from being on the outside of society looking in. Efforts toward reducing poverty are not necessary. What is required is that these people do what they need to do so that they can lift themselves above their current circumstances. The concept of poverty in the US and around the world is not new, but there has been an increase in the numbers of poor over time.

How do various institutions measure the poor, and what do their measurements mean? It might be the case that no one is really poor and that using a very liberal definition of what it means to be in poverty might be the issue. If someone is told that they are poor, then they will believe it. So we should have precise definitions of what it means when we say that someone is poor or that they are lower on the economic ladder. One simple way to measure poverty would be to set a relative scale. One that is commonly used states that earners who have household incomes below the 20% threshold are poor. This means that if we lined up all incomes in a country, from lowest to highest, and then measured the number of people who fell below the 20th percent level, we would call them the poor. In this way, the percentage of people not poor would remain constant at 80%, even though the numbers of people in each group would fluctuate. It is a clean metric and fairly easy to calculate, since any census of national income or earnings can be stacked and measured. If we used this scale measure, the percentage of people in poverty would never rise above 20%. However, even this metric can be rather deceiving when thought of in terms of people. For example, in 1922, there were approximately 110 million people living in the United States. Using the simple 20% poverty threshold, this would translate to around 22 million poor people. Some might argue that 22 million is an extremely large number and a source of concern. However, by 2022, the population had risen to 333 million people, a threefold increase, and so this crude 20% poverty metric would translate to 66.6 million people classified as poor. That would mean that even though the poverty rate never changed over those 100 years and remained constant at 20%, by 2022 every person in the states of Texas, Florida, and Pennsylvania could be counted as poor, with room to spare. Maybe society should think about a different way of measuring poverty, since the addition of over 40 million individuals to the poverty rolls seems problematic, even if it could be correctly stated that the poverty rate never moved over that period. What is interesting is that the official number of persons in poverty in the United States in 2021 was almost 40 million people, which translated to 11.6%. The number of people in poverty has actually been higher in the past, so some amount of concern seems warranted, even if we think all these people have chosen to be where they are or have a pathology or culture of dependency.

Given this backdrop, it might be worthwhile to explore how the poverty threshold was created for the United States in the first place and note that each country has its own definitions and metrics. One place to begin this exploration would be at the White House back in 1964, when President Lyndon Johnson declared the War on Poverty. It would be difficult to have a war without knowing the location, size, and persistence of the enemy, which would mean that some type of surveillance would be in order. This type of counting of the poor had not been done in any systematic way before then. Fortunately for the president, Mollie Orshansky, a social science research analyst working at the Social Security Administration, had begun to tackle this issue as far back as 1959.

By 1963, Orshansky had developed a threshold measure of poverty, which was adopted by the Office of Economic Opportunity as the official poverty measure for the United States in 1965.[1] This measure assumed that all individuals living in a household together shared income. Remember that in the first chapter I stated society was able to put aside considerations for those who, through no fault of their own, could not be expected to provide for themselves, like children or widows. By measuring poverty at the household level, society can alleviate concern about the unfortunate individual. After all, some individuals in the household could take advantage of the social contract and provide for others living there. As such, there was no need to provide much charity to individuals on the outside looking in. The measure assumes that individuals who were related by birth, marriage, or adoption and living in the same household spent a third of their income on food, so the plan estimated a "minimum food diet" in 1963 dollars. Once the cost of this minimum food diet was known, a researcher could simply multiply that number by three and set this income level as the threshold. An income below that amount would mean that these individuals were poor, because any number less than the threshold meant that the household was spending more than a third of their income on the minimum amount of food necessary to live.[2] The measure was adjusted for family size, given that the same amount of income meant different things for a mother and father with four children as opposed to a single female. Economists call these equivalence scales.

We should probably pause here to consider what the term *income* really means in this context. For the official measurement of poverty, it includes cash income, which can come from wages or salaries, Social Security benefits, interest, dividends, or retirement income. The distinction is important, because a tax accountant might scoff at the notion that these are the only sources of income a household could have. Clearly, there is a difference between this income definition and the one for taxable income.

With all this information in hand, in 1967 the US Census Bureau published its first set of poverty estimates for the US (Figure 2). It was only two years later that the Office of Management and Budget charged the Census Bureau with producing an "official" measure of poverty on an annual basis. Over the years there have been attempts to revise this measure by various scholars and institutions. Some of these revision efforts have been internal to the government, while researchers from academia have also taken on the task. In 1974, the government put together an interagency poverty studies task force headed by the Department of Health and Human Services. In 1992, the National Academy of Science convened a panel of experts to conduct a statistical review of problems with the official measure.[3] Some scrutiny of the measure does make sense. The poverty measure is problematic if its definition of the household is limited to only include those who are related by birth, marriage, or adoption. What about unmarried partners and their families, foster children, or coresident unrelated children? The dynamics of what constitutes a household and who lives together as a household unit has changed a great deal in the past 60 years. Plus, just measuring food needs seems shortsighted. There should be some accounting for clothing,

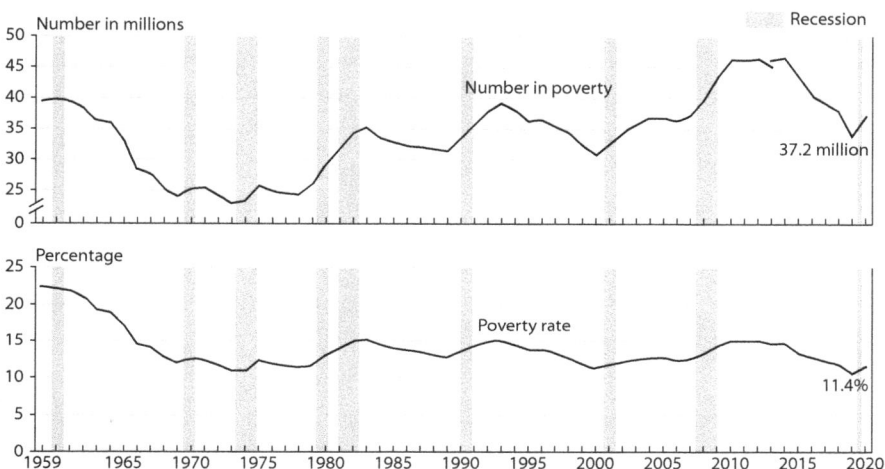

Figure 2. Number in poverty and poverty rate, 1959–2020. *Source:* Creamer et al., *Poverty in the United States: 2021,* citing data from U.S. Census Bureau, Current Population Survey, 1960 to 2021, Annual Social and Economic Supplements (CPS, ASEC).

shelter, utilities, and telecommunications. And if there is an accounting for only minimal food costs, what does a nutritional meal mean today compared to what was considered healthy then? There was a time in this country when smoking cigarettes was seen as a harmless hobby and cocaine was included in Coca-Cola. The official measure of poverty also does not account for the cost of living and has one national threshold, which makes little sense given that minimum costs in New York or Chicago will be vastly different from those in Omaha or Tuscaloosa. There should be some accounting for what helps people out of poverty, like tax credits, free lunch programs, housing subsidies, and so on, and accounting of those factors that pull people into poverty, like medical expenses (which will be discussed more in the next chapter), payroll taxes, transportation to and from work, and so on.[4] Given all these concerns, the Bureau of Labor Statistics and the Census Bureau joined forces to create the

Supplemental Poverty Measure in 2009. For the past 60 years, the United States has endeavored to have a fairly accurate picture of the number and percentage of Americans in poverty. The measure might not capture every aspect of poverty, but it has been consistently measured. That point of consistency is important if the reader is to get an apples-to-apples portrait of how things have progressed with regard to poverty over the past six decades.

OTHER POVERTY METRICS

In some countries or regions of the world, the poverty metric is a percentage of the mean, or average income. In this case, if the average income is rising in a country, then the threshold for poverty will rise by that rate also. After all, why should the poverty metric only rise with inflation? If the average citizen of the country is doing better, should not society expect some of that benefit to be shared with those less fortunate? If society believes that economic growth and benefit should be expected to reach those at the lower end of the income strata, then this type of indexing makes some sense. If society believes that the poor will realize little if any of that gain, then an inflation-adjusted measure probably makes more sense. We often see economic policies touted as being good for all people on the income ladder, but if that is so, then all people should be moving in terms of their income gains. These differences matter when considering what form of poverty metric to design and use.

There is good work being done on the international side of poverty investigations too. The United Nations (UN) has set a goal of eradicating poverty by the year 2030.[5] However, this is not the first said proclamation by this group, or others, over time. Individual societies and the world in general have to ask themselves this question: Are we getting any closer to these lofty goals, or are we just kicking the can down the road? What we can say at this point is that the UN relies on the World Bank for its data calculations of the number of people around the globe who fall below the international poverty line (IPL).

What exactly is the IPL and why is it used? Is it like the official poverty line that the US uses? The short answer is no—it is not even close to the US measure of poverty. The World Bank sets the IPL so that it is representative of the various national poverty definitions that have been adopted by the world's poorest countries. In September of 2022, the IPL was raised from $1.90 to $2.15 per day.[6] This number of $2 a day is commonly used in the press, even though the number never was set exactly at $2. The change reflected the change in the units that the World Bank uses to express poverty and inequality. Previously, they were indexed by international dollars reflected in 2011 prices but were updated to 2017 prices. That move up to $2.15 in international dollars was needed as an attempt to stay current with ever-increasing prices of goods. In the next decade there will probably need to be another adjustment, given the rapid rise in inflation that occurred after the COVID-19 pandemic. At this point, you might be asking: What exactly are international dollars?

When dealing with data about income inequality or inflation or goods and services bought or sold, the normal unit of measure is the local currency where the transaction took place. For example, most of the eurozone would record transactions in euros and the United States uses US dollars. The problem is that inflation over time makes comparisons difficult even with the same unit of currency. When a transaction is recorded at a given time in a given currency, it is normally referred to as being in *nominal*, or current, prices. There needs to be a common way to compare the same good across time and across countries. This commonality is especially critical for any meaningful discussion of world poverty. Is a five-pound bag of rice purchased in 2019 in Kampala, Uganda, the same as a five-pound bag of rice purchased in 2023 in Kabul, Afghanistan?

An international dollar is designed to act as a hypothetical currency that would allow for the purchase of the same good over time and across countries. When the World Bank changed the year of indexing from 2011 to 2017, it actually did two things. This move allowed for purchasing happening around the world to be linked to prices in 2017, so any inflation occurring going forward would be compared to base price levels in 2017. This is easier and more convenient for the user. Imagine using prices in the United States from the year 1930, when a gallon of milk was 26 cents, to try to purchase a car in 2025. A great deal of mental gymnastics would be needed to make any meaningful use of the value of a dollar from long ago, today. That is why we move the reference year forward periodically. Comparing prices between 2020 and 2022 is much easier than comparing those between 1952 and 2022. In addition, the world must be concerned with something economists call *purchasing power parity*, which equates prices across the globe. The same item might have vastly different prices in other countries, even after accounting for exchanging a foreign currency for the local currency. With these international dollars, the World Bank can make reasonable comparisons about needed items over time and place. With this set, the goal of figuring out the IPL, which was the ultimate goal, becomes more tenable.[7]

We've spent a great deal of time in this chapter explaining how the United States calculates poverty and the history of that outcome. All countries do some variation of that procedure, and the World Bank uses a representative of the poorest countries for world poverty measures. It would make little sense to include countries like the United States or Germany in such measures, as they would only distort the true picture of global disparity. In other words, the $2 a day metric would be distorted if we included the US, since its poverty rate would be dramatically lower than that of other countries around the world (Figure 3).

And what are the results of global poverty before and after that World Bank update? The answer is that not much changed regarding the number of people globally living in extreme poverty. In 1990, under the $1.90 per day metric, 36.29% of the world population (1.92 billion people) was living in extreme poverty. Under the revised

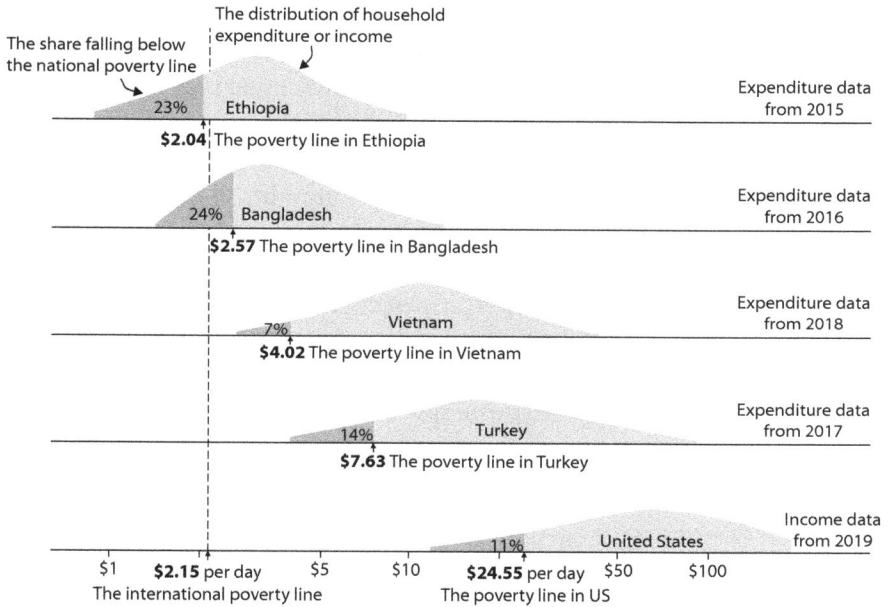

Figure 3. National poverty lines, poverty rates, and incomes in five countries. Those living on less than $2.15 per day are considered by the UN definition to be in extreme poverty. In Ethiopia, 23% of people are below the national poverty line of $2.04 and therefore also in extreme poverty; an additional small percentage of Ethiopians live above the national poverty line but still below the international poverty line. In Bangladesh, 24% of people are below the national poverty line of $2.57, with some but not all these individuals in extreme poverty. For Vietnam (7% of people below the national poverty line of $4.02), Turkey (14% of people below the national poverty line of $7.63), and the United States (11% of people below the national poverty line of $24.55), nobody living in national poverty is also in extreme poverty. *Source:* Hasell et al., "Poverty," citing data from Jolliffe (2022), U.S. Census Bureau, and World Bank Poverty and Inequality Platform.

$2.15 per day metric, those 1990 numbers would have been 37.81% of the world population (2.0 billion people) living in extreme poverty. By 2019, the numbers had decreased dramatically to 8.7% (668.2 million people) using the $1.90 measure, as opposed to 8.44% (648.1 million people) using the $2.15 measure.[8]

Why do the United States and the rest of the world spend such a great deal of effort to identify so precisely the number of poor and the levels of inequality in the world? I would argue that the world, including the United States, has a high tolerance for poverty and inequality, because many can console themselves with the idea that these people in poverty are where they want to be. The road map is laid out for them to leave their current situation and assume a spot next to those who have plenty. If these two-billion-plus individuals would only embrace the social contract, they would not be where they are. Therefore, they must want to be there, or they have a pathology that prevents them from going any higher. This view is supported by example after example of rags to riches stories broadcast on television, told in the popular press, and, more than ever, influenced by social media.

INCOME INEQUALITY

Many scholars have stated that income inequality, or income disparity, is actually a good sign. They argue that this inequality shows that innovators and first movers, or rather risk-takers, are getting out front and taking risks to bring new products and services to market. They would put up as proof of concept all the inventions, technologies, and services that have benefited society since humans first invented the wheel. Where would we be as a world without these entrepreneurs? The argument goes that these inventors took the majority of the risks and thus should be rewarded with the majority of the benefits. It is natural then to see economic inequality, which separates the risk-taking individual from those not willing to "build a better mousetrap." However, the argument does not end there, as these same scholars posit that this inequality is only a temporary blip. Eventually, the new products and services that made some individuals rich will filter down through society and everyone will have access to them, raising the standard of living for all. For example, think of the personal computer, which made Bill Gates and Steve Jobs billionaires many times over. The personal computer is now so ubiquitous that more computing power is found in a cheap smart phone than in the first Intel 386 and 486 32-bit microprocessors, which were considered cutting-edge, state-of-the-art computers in the mid-1980s. These new products and services can now be used to create the next iteration of upwardly mobile entrepreneurs, thus closing the inequality gap even more.

The most well-known hypothesis of inequality and economic growth was posited by Simon Kuznets in the mid-1950s.[9] There have been thousands of scholarly papers written using the "Kuznets hypothesis." Kuznets put forth the idea that there was very little inequality in countries with very low per capita income and countries with very high per capita income. There would be rising and then falling levels of inequality for countries in the middle. If this curve was drawn as a graph, with per capita income along the horizontal axis and income inequality along the vertical axis, it would be a round hump (Figure 4).

The argument used by Kuznets was that subsistence existence in poor or developing countries primarily revolves around agricultural production. This type of production creates a relatively equal playing field and there is little inequality. In essence, everyone was rather poor and there was little that could distinguish one poor farmer from another, given that the weather one experienced was about the same for their neighbor. At some point, some farmers or their children became merchants and moved to towns or villages, which grew to be urban areas. Urbanization creates the need for more workers, and this increase in demand for workers leads to higher wages, inducing more individuals to leave the farm and become industrialized workers. Given the time when Kuznets was writing, it is easy to see how he came to such conclusions. In 1920, the census showed that the farm population of the US was slightly over 30%. By 1986, that number had dropped to 2.2%.[10] People clearly had left the farm in droves and gone to the city. Correspondingly, the differences in

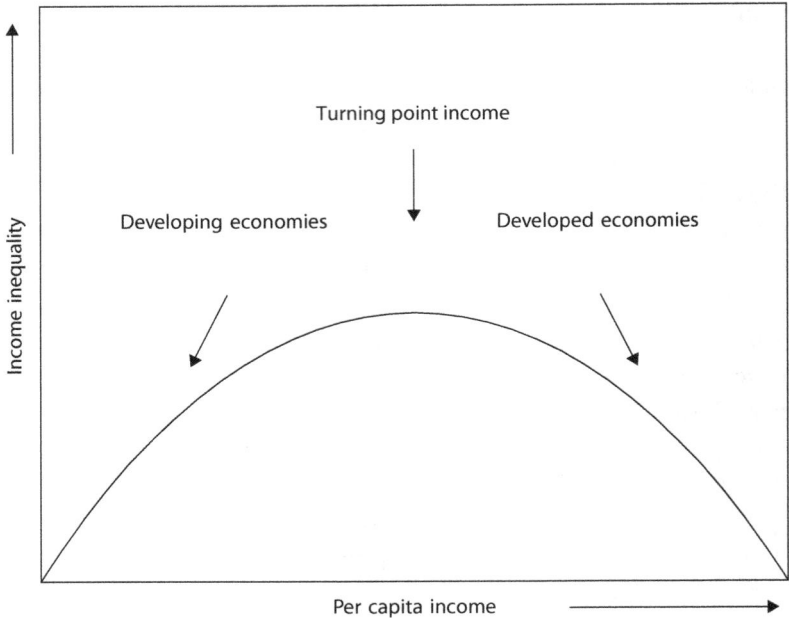

Figure 4. Depiction of the Kuznets curve, showing increasing then decreasing inequality as countries increase per capita incomes. *Source:* Created by author.

wealth and income became more pronounced over time, and inequality along with per capita income began to rise, according to the theory due to this migration. However, there will come a point when the benefits of modernization and industrialization will raise the standard of living for all, including those on the farm, given the dispersion of goods and services brought to market for the benefit of the entire society. As the conveniences of new goods and services trickle down throughout society, there should be a decrease in economic differences coinciding with an increase in per capita income.

There is a problem with this idea, given that since the 1960s inequality has risen most and fastest in developed countries—in other words, in high per capita income countries like the United States. The hump shape of the Kuznets curve no longer holds, but the idea that we can have it all, where there will be higher per capita income for all and less inequality, persists as those individuals at the bottom continue to remain faithful to the tenets of the social contract. Basically, the idea is that "a rising tide lifts all boats" and failures—that is, poverty—are the result of a lack of seaworthiness of some vessels.

Thus far, I have mainly centered on understanding the numbers and levels of disparity of those at the bottom of the income spectrum—those considered in poverty. It makes sense, given that protests about actions taken but not resulting in desired outcomes are most likely to arise from this group.

It should be noted that the poor are not the only ones who could rightfully claim their actions did not result in upward mobility. This is why I have refrained from referring to the "undeserving poor" but rather just those who see themselves as undeserving. It does make sense to think more broadly of those who might make the claim that the social contract has failed them if we focus our attention on income inequality, which Table 1 will be helpful in doing.

Imagine that society has 100 people and $100 that is to be distributed to the populous. One way of distributing the income is to give each person $1. Now imagine further that we separate the population into groups of 20 people. We now have five groups, with each group having 20 people. In sticking with our original plan, we could give each group of 20 people $20 to share among themselves. This would result in each person having $1.

But given that we have the perfectly functioning social contract and starting position is not that important, what we could do is give the lowest group of 20 people only $4.10 to share among themselves. That would equate to each person in this group having a little over 20 cents. On the other end, we could take the 20 people in the highest group and give them $43.30 to share. This would equate to each person in this group having approximately $2.16. Each person in this group would have over half of what the entire lowest 20 people had in their group, combined.

Table 1   Shares of income in the US in 1970 and 2022

	Lowest 20%	Second-lowest 20%	Middle 20%	Second-highest 20%	Highest 20%
1970	4.1%	10.8%	17.4%	24.5%	43.3%
2022	3.5%	9.1%	14.6%	22.1%	50.7%

SOURCE: United States Census Bureau, "Historical Income Tables: Households."

The numbers in Table 1 come directly from the US Census Bureau and show how income was distributed in the country over a 52-year period. In 1970, the lowest 20% of the US population had 4.1% of the income and the highest 20% of the population had 43.3% of all the income in the country. It is clear to see that income was not evenly distributed back then.

The next logical question is, how have things progressed since then? The second row of the table shows that things have become even more unequal. Where the lowest 20% of the population had 4.1% of the income in 1970, that share dropped to 3.5% in 2022. Those at the top of the income scale have done better, given that from 1970 to 2022, the share of income held by the top 20% increased from 43.3% to 50.7%. Over half of all the income in the country was held by 20% of the population.

By examining the table, we can see that every group except the highest has lost ground regarding their share of income over the 52-year period. That includes the middle class, which is considered the cornerstone of a stable economy and society.

This simple chart comes with a few caveats that need mentioning, such as the fact that this is a chart of before-tax income. Given that taxes are redistributed from the higher income group to the lower, the amount of income that each group has is not truly reflected in this chart. In addition, it is a chart of income and not wealth, meaning that it does not account for substantial holdings that people in a group might have. There are other things to consider, but I will also note that this table is not dynamic, by which I mean that people have moved up and down the chart over the period, and new people have entered the economy while others have left. It is not clear that the group comprising the lowest 20% are the same people. However, this chart is telling in that there is no denying that the rich got richer, no matter who they were.

Those who believe in the social contract argue that there is no real reason to be terribly concerned that there are so many poor people, even though this chapter has spent a great deal of time quantifying how we count this particular group. They would argue that they are there by their own hands, and moreover, adherence to the social contract will lift them out of their current situation if and when they are willing to apply themselves. This is not a new idea. In 1969, David Landes stated, "Where once poverty had been looked on as an unavoidable evil and the poor man as an object of pity and a responsibility to his neighbor, now poverty was a sin and poor man a victim of his own iniquity."[11]

In 2022, Jon Wisman made an even more interesting observation and tied in the ideas of history and the Protestant work ethic. His thesis was that merchants in the Middle Ages had been able to acquire some measure of wealth through commerce. With this new wealth came the hope of attaining higher social status, which had been reserved for those of noble birth. He states,

> The bourgeoisie's quest for status and self-respect help explain the success of the Protestant Reformation. This religious revolution supplied legitimacy to wealth acquired through individual achievement. It is through the Protestant virtues of hard work and asceticism that the bourgeoisie earned its wealth. And in lacking these virtues, the slothfulness of the poor earned them poverty. Status came progressively to be seen less as given by birth and more as the result of performance or achievement, although the pinnacle of status

long remained grounded in aristocratic birth. Since the 1950s, achievement-based status has come to be called meritocracy.[12]

With our advances in data sciences and algorithmic inference, countries around the globe are able to calculate with a great deal of accuracy how many people are left behind. As mentioned previously, society is absolved of caring beyond a very basic humanitarian level by inserting the surety of the social contract, and words like *merit-based achievement, entrepreneurship*, and *personal responsibility* are where some would argue our focus should be. Keep in mind the idea of pathology. Ron Haskins has said that "opportunity in America depends largely on decisions made by people who are free actors. . . . Unless young Americans begin making better decisions, the nation's problems with poverty and inequality will continue to grow. . . . Yes, the nation needs its safety net, but improvements in personal responsibility would have a greater and more lasting impact on poverty and opportunity."[13]

It is not surprising that protests have erupted over the decades on a variety of fronts by individuals who want to clearly distinguish themselves from those in society "deserving" of their lower economic status. The undeserving could state, "I might be among these people who are poor, but I am not a part of them." Future chapters will show that as the group of individuals who state "I should not be here!" grows to a tipping point among the lower-income parts of society, there will be some form of unrest.

Per Alesina et al., "Sixty percent of American respondents, but only 26 percent of Europeans, say that the poor are lazy."[14] In the United States, it is widely believed the poor are impacted by their own laziness. There has been real resentment from some undeserving individuals about being cast in with those deemed to be neglectful of their responsibilities to the social contract caused by their own inadequacy, but there is also resentment from those legitimately in need of help. It is echoed in the refrain "no one helped me." In a scholarly article written by Alesina and La Ferrara in 2001, the authors reported that individuals in the US who believed they were going to see some future income growth were less inclined to support any type of redistributive efforts toward the poorer members of society.[15] This implies that those at the lower rungs of the income distribution would rather go without assistance now so that if they ever rise above their current circumstances, they will not be asked to help others. The refrain heard most often is "I made it here without help from anyone." The idea of explicit help given to certain cohorts or demographics of the population is effrontery, given the existence of a social contract.

What I have shown in this chapter is that the United States and the rest of the world have a fairly accurate account of how poverty is measured across the globe and the number of people who are poor, along with the magnitude of the gap between them and others higher up on the economic and social ladder. All these advanced calculations and investigations to understand the numbers matter in a real sense. Policymakers in society might or might not be inclined to take action on behalf of those whom I have termed undeserving of their status if the numbers do not add up. It really depends on how many individuals are undeserving. Is it 1 out of every 1,000 lower-rung individuals? What if it is one in one million? Clearly, policymakers could rightly argue that the social contract works, on average, or even for almost all. Changing policy for one out of a million seems very costly. We better spend a good deal of time understanding the numbers and the nature of the problem. Society might also want to refrain from claiming that those in lower positions are simply choosing their station in life.

No matter how we measure those at lower positions, some will argue that they should not be there. Some will argue that they are not "poor" as defined by any of the metrics that have been examined but still occupy a rung on the economic ladder below the level that they feel their actions have warranted. Later chapters will detail why they feel that way and what they did to let that fact be known. This chapter has detailed how we measure poverty and inequality so that the reader might, once again, ponder the central question that drove me to write this book. Namely, are there really over two billion people on this planet who simply are "fleas" or lazy or suffering from some form of cultural malaise that keeps them from taking the necessary actions to climb above their current situation? And what about those who have tried to take the actions their society has deemed as appropriate to rise above their current circumstances, only to be met with disappointment?

3 Social Contracts in Theory and Practice

In this chapter, I will lay out a few examples of social contracts and how they theoretically should operate and lead to assured upward mobility for those who engage in the society-endorsed actions prescribed. These activities are what upper-income individuals can point to when confronted by those who are at a lower, and sometimes significantly lower, rung of the economic and social ladder. Instead of providing some form of charity to those in poverty, upper-income individuals are able to ask whether these people have truly embraced these activities before asking for assistance. However, in many cases what I show is that the actual execution of the action does not live up to the expectations of universal upward mobility for all, regardless of their starting place on the economic or social scale. If this is truly a ladder and the rung is there, maybe it is not as close to the one above as was believed and people spend energy reaching for it but never grabbing it. As mentioned previously, if several individuals do the exact same activity yet one person has a dramatically different result, then our social contract might best be described as a lottery instead of a ladder.

In the next few chapters, I will go even further, with a few examples to show how citizens can become disillusioned with the social contract and consider themselves as undeserving of their position in society. In certain cases, once a large enough number of these individuals coalesce, there can be a tipping or inflection point where protest arises. What will also be interesting to investigate is when society agrees with the self-assessment of these individuals and when it does not.

EDUCATION

To begin with, the most commonly mentioned and easily recognizable social contract is education. The premise is clear: If someone engages in this self-improving and society-endorsed activity, then a higher rung on the economic and social ladder will be the result. Education at the K–12 level is clearly strongly encouraged by society, given that it is free and compulsory in the United States and many other nations around the world. There are child labor laws to protect children from early exits from the school system and into the workforce. The rationale for such prudence is that having children in school will provide long-term benefits for them and for society that surpass the short-term gains of immediate employment.

What has given the United States the highest standard of living across the globe? Many would argue that it has been the embrace of public education. By the 1840s, the US had high primary school enrollments per capita, surpassing some European countries. Literacy rates among the free population were exceptionally high.[1] There was an undeniable link between an educated citizenry and economic innovation and productivity. With the educational system being highly decentralized, there was the opportunity for rapid diffusion of information that was tailored to the local community. Where some nations had educational systems approaching a one-size-fits-all model, the US had a great deal of educational variety in instruction.

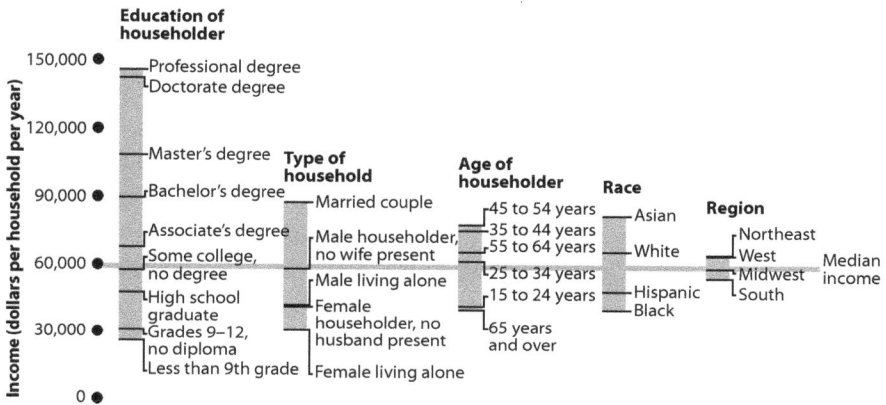

Figure 5. The distribution of income by selected household characteristics. *Source:* Parkin, *Microeconomics*, chap. 19, fig. 2.

(Some would argue that this decentralization has led to many of the problems that the educational system currently faces with regard to funding, and we will discuss this in more depth later on.)

This system of education had great advantages. After publicly funded primary schools were established, girls received an education that was similar to the one boys received, and by the middle of the 20th century a greater fraction of girls attended and graduated from secondary schools.[2] It is clear that during the late 19th century to the middle of the 20th century, the US was a leader in education, which also coincided with great technological and innovative advances for the economy and the standard of living for most households. Economists and historians refer to some of this period as the Industrial Revolution, given how new techniques in manufacturing and engineering were being implemented. Educating large masses of students met the definition of the social contract, in that both individuals and society benefited from these actions.

Figure 5 is very revealing in several dimensions. The figure shows that the median income in the United States in 2016 was about

$60,000. This number exactly split all households in the United States, meaning that 50% of households had incomes below this number and 50% were above. If we examine educational attainment, we see that there is a sizeable gap between those households led by individuals with educational attainment less than an associate's degree. Having only completed the ninth grade or completed high school results in incomes in the lower half. On the other hand, having any form of advanced degree, from an associate's degree up to a doctorate, puts households in the upper half. If one thinks of education as a vehicle toward upward mobility, then this graph seems to add credibility to that argument. This would appear to be a social contract working as intended, with clear benefits for all. What must be stressed here and with other statistics in this graph is that being below the median does not necessarily mean that the household is in poverty. The very reason the household might be lower on the economic spectrum but not in poverty could be the embrace of the society-endorsed activity of educating themselves. In other words, someone with a high school diploma might not be in the upper half of income earners but not in poverty precisely because they have the diploma instead of having left high school early.

The decentralization of the K–12 educational system did lead to an ability to quickly disperse information, but it also has given rise to disparities that make the quality of the education received very uneven across the country. This unevenness gives rise to faults in the social contract, if education is believed to be a key driver of upward mobility. The issue mostly revolves around funding. In some school districts, and sometimes particular schools within a district, the access to technology can be stark. In some schools, each child has their own iPad or Chromebook to work on and take home to complete assignments, while other schools have fewer, older devices that are not allowed to leave the classroom. To say these students have all received the same level of training would be erroneous, even though it can truthfully be stated that they all had access to advanced technology.

The disparities in the quality of the educational experience extend to the environment where learning is to take place, given that some school districts are unable to fix old school buildings or the heating and air conditioning units in them. In some districts, there is not enough funding to hire additional teachers so that class sizes can be reduced, or hire teachers skilled enough to provide for students with language gaps, or hire other support staff needed for a variety of issues.

The zip code in which a student lives can explain a great deal about the level of funding provided to the school districts. Local property taxes make up the majority of the funding strategy used in this decentralized system. The following excerpt from an article written for *AP News* perfectly encapsulates the problem, describing the funding differences between two neighboring school districts in Pennsylvania.

> Consider that Allentown spent about $14,854 to educate each of its students in the 2017–18 school year, with about 33% of it coming from local taxes. In the neighboring Salisbury Township School District, $22,841 was spent on each student, with 73% coming from local taxes.
>
> Local taxes alone generated $16,666 for each Salisbury student, surpassing the revenue Allentown received from local, state and federal sources combined. Adding state and federal money to the equation, Salisbury had $8,000 more to spend on each of its students than Allentown had.
>
> Drawing a correlation between Allentown's financial state and the quality of education it can provide, Parker wrote in an opinion piece in *The Morning Call* in May: "It cannot be the narrative of this city, this region, this district, that Allentown students somehow deserve less."[3]

The success or failings of education as a society-endorsed activity might lie in the true purpose of public education. Is the purpose of schooling to prepare young minds for the adult workforce? There was a time when young people sat and learned in the shops of master craftsmen as apprentices. Is mass education just a scaling up of trade guilds? It could be the case that schooling creates citizens who are better capable of participating in society and, even more so, in a democracy where voting regarding the direction of the country takes place and a better informed electorate is more likely to engage in the democratic process. This idea would see young people learning for learning's sake and not for any particular application in the economy. These questions do not have to be either/or propositions, and the purpose of public education could be to accomplish both of these goals and more, but society will have to think hard about how this was achieved in the past and how it will be achieved in the future.

One other thing that is missing from this story of a functioning social contract is the ever-rising cost of a college education. As mentioned in Chapter 1, the costs of engaging the social contract have to be considered if society is going to tout this activity as one assuring those who are lower on the economic and social ladder upward mobility. A 2023 *Forbes* article analyzed data from the National Center for Education Statistics.[4] It reported that in 1980 the cost of attending a four-year college full-time was $10,231. Disturbingly, by 2019–20 that cost, which was inflation adjusted, had risen to $28,775. That was an increase of 180%, which far outpaced the rate of inflation experienced over the same period. What was even more alarming was that a private, nonprofit college had annual tuition fees of $48,965 in 2019–20, compared to $21,035 for a public university. These types of prices could be the reason that college education has become increasingly unattainable for those at the lower range of the income spectrum. As mentioned earlier, in 2016, $19,105 was the poverty threshold for a family of three. If those at the bottom of the income distribution are the ones most in need of taking advantage of this activity, then prices that restrict their access might call for a rethinking of how to operationalize this endeavor. Obviously, borrowing for college has always been an option for potential students. In economics, scholars often mention the idea of income smoothing, where early in life individuals take on debt that allows them to attain a higher lifetime earnings path later on. As a result, they are able to pay back the borrowed resources and maintain a higher standard of living than they would have without borrowing and investing in themselves. Later, in Chapter 7, I will discuss in great detail the perils and resentment caused by borrowing for a college education. I will show how a sizeable group of people have coalesced around the idea of these costs being a violation of the social contract and how they have voiced their resentment.

So, how well the practice of education as a social contract activity matches the theory is debatable. It could be troubling if a social contract activity does not work for the entire society. People will come to rely on the certainty of the activity, and if it does not live up to expectations, there might be resentment. This is where people might come to see education as being a gamble, or a lottery, instead of a ladder. The idea of a tipping point of people who feel they are undeserving of their station becomes more plausible when obvious gaps between theory and practice exist.

HEALTH CARE

Another interesting social contract is that of health, or healthy living. Admittedly, there is no real agreement in an increasingly polarized society about what a healthy lifestyle means. For the purposes of what I will discuss, the term that best describes this activity might actually be *health care*. The social contract would state that individuals should do all they can to avoid unnecessary risks and live as healthy as possible. The benefit to the individual is rather obvious: Hopefully they will have a better quality of life, no matter what their occupation is, or if they are employed at all. These individuals will also find that living healthily is cost-efficient for them, given the high cost of health care after injury or illness. That is not to say there are no costs involved in taking care of oneself both mentally and physically, but the costs of preventive care generally pale in comparison to the costs after an injury or illness. By one estimate, in 2016, the

United States spent a staggering $730.4 billion on preventable ill-nesses.[5] In addition, the range of employment opportunities expands immensely for those who have the physical and mental ability to engage in certain occupations. Think of firefighters or police officers as examples of jobs requiring a minimum level of health and fitness.

The social contract would state that these healthy individuals put themselves at an advantage over their less healthy peers and have greater opportunities for upward mobility, both socially and eco-nomically, as a result. The healthy person will have higher self-esteem and be more engaged in activities of importance to them. The amount of time and effort needed to maintain the body and mind will be minimal compared to the time needed to rehabilitate after illness or injury, or the time needed to maintain health for those with low health markers, like obesity or smoking.

Society benefits from healthy individuals and communities because they tend to be more productive and thus more prosperous. In a 2022 study by the National Bureau of Economic Research, researchers found that better health increased labor market partici-pation and worker productivity. The authors state that "better health, particularly that of women, reduces fertility and spurs an economic transition from a state of stagnating incomes toward sus-tained economic growth."[6]

Better health outcomes seem to generate many societal benefits. Those researchers also mentioned that they calculated something called the "survival rate," which is akin to life expectancy, and found that for every 10% increase in the adult survival rate, there is a 10.6% increase in worker productivity. It should not come as a surprise that healthier citizens will live longer and be more productive in their jobs. Reports show that a great deal of cross-country differences in per worker incomes can be traced to population health. In this situ-ation, a social contract that supports and encourages greater indi-vidual health outcomes will foster greater economic growth for all.

In my time as a professor of economics, I have had occasion to speak with business owners from a variety of areas of the business world.

When they have been asked what they want from a local labor force, their answers have been rather consistent. They would like the labor force to be trainable, or in other words, they are looking for an educable workforce. The other point often made by managers and business owners is that they would prefer a workforce that will be at their jobs consistently. This means that the levels of absenteeism will be minimal. One of the greatest reasons employees miss work is due to illness or other health-related issues. A 2022 *Forbes* article stated, "Injuries, illness and medical appointments are the most commonly reported reasons for missing work (though not always the actual reason). Not surprisingly, each year during the cold and flu season, there is a dramatic spike in absenteeism rates for both full-time and part-time employees."[7] The costs of absenteeism are not small, and employers lose billions of dollars in productivity annually due to sick workers.

It seems clear that keeping all citizens up and down the economic and social ladder healthy should be a very high priority for society. The end result of these encouragements would be to get more people into the workforce and get greater productivity out of those already working. Theoretically, this social contract makes a great deal of sense. However, in practice, there are many shortcomings of the contract that could lead people to consider themselves to be undeserving of their status. In other words, the health care ladder might have damaged, missing, or misaligned rungs.

The problem with health and many other activities as social contracts is that after engaging in the society-endorsed activity, the citizen is expecting to be better off socially or financially than when they began. With health and health care, as it is currently administered in the US, it is possible for an individual to have lived as healthy a lifestyle as they possibly could but have one medical emergency that drops them lower, sometimes much lower, on the economic and social ladder than their starting position. In essence, they have regressed despite their diligent efforts, which might result in resentment.

The fact that the modern lexicon has the term *medical bankruptcy* is indicative of the failings of a health-focused social contract. While writing this chapter, I typed the term *medical bankruptcy* into my computer search engine and got no fewer than eight pages of websites devoted to every aspect of how one navigates this issue. In its simplest form, an individual incurs so much debt from medical bills, which have not or cannot be paid, they have to seek financial protection from the courts. These enormous medical debts can be incurred by the "deserving," meaning those who did very little, if anything, to live a healthy lifestyle, for instance, by using illegal drugs or ignoring advice from medical professionals. However, such debts can also be incurred by those individuals who did, indeed, do all that they were advised to do to live a healthy existence. These individuals would certainly classify themselves as being undeserving of their plight. Given that any type of bankruptcy will impact credit scores, which, in turn, could limit the individual's ability to move up the economic ladder, it would be distressing to some to find themselves unable to cover medical debts.

What makes this situation of medical bankruptcy more egregious is that many individuals had full-time employment that came with medical benefits. Consider this headline from *The Guardian*, a British newspaper: "'I Live on the Street Now': How Americans Fall into Medical Bankruptcy."[8] The article describes a situation that is all too familiar. A woman named Susanne LeClair of West Palm Beach, Florida, who was employed full-time and had health insurance through her employer, was diagnosed with cancer. She went to the hospital to receive treatment; however, the trauma of cancer was not enough. She was also saddled with hundreds of thousands of dollars of medical bills afterward, which her insurance did not cover. She had no alternative but to declare bankruptcy.

The story goes on to detail that she tried to pay for drugs that were needed for her recovery through a maze of transferring debt from one credit card to another. She also had fears that she might end up needing to file for bankruptcy a second time. Lest we think this is a person who simply had poor financial skills or wanted to be in the situation she found herself in, the article states that "one out of every six Americans has an unpaid medical bill on their credit report, amounting to $81bn in debt nationwide, while about one in 12 Americans went without any medical insurance throughout 2018."[9] This appears to be much more than a one-off occurrence of an individual with bad luck. "A lot of people, a little over 60%, are filing bankruptcy at least in part because of medical bills. Most of them are insured. It's clear that despite health insurance, there are many, many people incurring costs not being covered by their insurance," said Dr. David Himmelstein, distinguished professor of public health at City University of New York's Hunter College and a lecturer in medicine at Harvard Medical School, who was quoted in this piece.

There has been discussion for a number of years about the state of the US health care system and there will be more discussion in Chapter 5, because the theory is not matching the practice. Clearly, to tout health as a society-endorsed activity in the social contract would require it to function for all (which it does not), and rather efficiently (which it has not).

FAMILY STRUCTURE

A 2021 headline on a financial planning website read, "Don't Become a Parent Until You've Hit These Money Milestones."[10] The message is clear: Those who are lower on the economic ladder should delay family formation, or at least having children, until their financial standing is higher up the ladder. This ideology might be seen as an inversion of the idea of a social contract where action results in benefit. In this case, one could think of inaction, that is, delaying children, as what leads to benefit. The social contract, as I have laid it out, would state here that individuals should engage in other society-endorsed activities to move up the economic and social ladder first, and then consider family planning. By doing so, these individuals would not risk placing themselves in peril by not having enough resources to rise above their current economic status, given that child-rearing can be a very expensive undertaking.

The social contract would state that individuals who wait to have children have also helped secure a better starting position for their offspring, given that the accumulated wealth of the family is sticky and intergenerationally transferable. The reason that society would endorse this course of action would be that the burden of caring for the well-being of these children would not be spread to others through government assistance programs for low-income families. There is a fairly common notion among some people that poor women, and particularly minority women, have children for the increase in state assistance that occurs with greater family size. It is a long-standing narrative. In 2012, *The New York Times* ran an obituary of James R. Dumpson, who had at one point been the commissioner of welfare for New York City. Sometime around 1959, Mr. Dumpson wrote a scathing response to an editorial run in the *Daily News*, with the headline: "Ladies Have Babies by Assorted Gentlemen So As to Keep the Relief Checks Growing Fatter Each Year."[11] This idea of family size creating a burden on society, crippling children to a life of dependency and hindering individuals from successfully engaging in society-endorsed activities, has been around for at least three-quarters of a century, if not longer.

There is some reasonableness for at least considering the timing of family formation. From Figure 5, seen earlier, we also learn that one of the things that separated households above and below the median income was the type of household. The term *householder* refers to a male or female who is a parent but lives alone with the children with no married partner. Caution should be taken, because being below the median income does not imply being in poverty, as I stated before. In addition, for women with children, their household income was greater than that of single women. This all is a snapshot, however, and if income mobility is greater for those who have more time to dedicate to activities prescribed by the social contract, then delaying family until a more substantial economic footing is established would seem advisable.

The notion that some poor and minority women have children to increase state assistance has been debunked in the past. Elon University has a Program for Ethnographic Research and Community Studies (PERCS), which partnered with community agencies to launch a multiyear, collaborative ethnographic research project that examined the perceptions and realities surrounding the welfare system. What they found was strong evidence of children not being a net financial gain for poor families. For instance, they report that in the state of North Carolina, a poor mother having an additional child would not receive large amounts of benefits. In fact, they state that "for each additional child, she would receive an average of $28 per month." Raising an additional child will surely cost more than $28 per month. Also, they report that food assistance, which used to commonly be known as food stamps, or Supplement Nutritional Assistance Program (SNAP), has marginal increases with additional children. As they state, "A new child could raise a family's SNAP benefits by $159 per month."[12]

The idea of delaying children or not having them at all seems to have resonated with a large portion of the US population. As the Pew Research Center reported in 2021, "Some 44% of non-parents ages 18 to 49 say it is not too or not at all likely that they will have children someday" and "74% of adults younger than 50 who are already parents say they are unlikely to have more kids."[13] Delaying or not having children was not primarily driven by financial considerations. The report stated, "Among those younger than 50 who say there was some other reason why they probably will not have more children, age (theirs or their partner's) and medical reasons were among the top reasons why (29% and 23% of this group said so, respectively), followed by financial reasons (14%)." We just covered health care as a social contract, so it is not surprising that this reason enters the list near the top.

As a young untenured assistant professor at the University of Alabama, I would occasionally have lunch with a friend who was a

Catholic priest. On occasion, we would discuss this idea of family formation among those who were fiscally unable to provide for their children and required assistance. If the social contract was to be believed, these individuals should have delayed such decisions until they had fully engaged in other society-endorsed activities, regardless of how many children were involved. My friend would admonish me for such thinking. The problem with this line of reasoning, as he put it, was that it separated these people from their humanity. In his words, economists had reduced childbearing to a production function, where a commodity (children) was produced. He would argue that one should never equate having children with something like going to buy a loaf of bread. He would say that all life, whether rich or poor, was precious and had dignity. The one thing that all humans were capable of doing across the globe and throughout history was to reproduce. He would go on to say that there are not many things that everyone has in common, but producing life was fundamentally written into our DNA and no amount of resources or social standing was going to stop people from being who they were.

The resentment from this social contract activity is clear and can be asked in one question: What if some people never rise to the "required" income level for children? The contract would say they should not be allowed to have children until they reach that money milestone, so those other activities better work or there will be fewer children. Will those individuals higher up on the economic ladder have enough children for the entirety of society? The theory of this activity is clear, but the practice is much more complicated.

ENTREPRENEURSHIP

There is a quote that is often attributed to Ralph Waldo Emerson, although he never actually said it: "Build a better mousetrap, and the world will beat a path to your door." The underlying and enduring power of the statement is that innovation and entrepreneurship is the key to economic success and upward mobility. For the purposes of this book, entrepreneurship can be seen as a social contract. The definitive action needed is creating a product or service and then bringing it to market. There should be a great deal of upward movement on the economic and social ladder, given the time and effort it takes to engage in, design, develop, and then produce and market new products and services. These businesses generally start out small and grow through the efforts and determination of their owners. According to the Small Business Administration (SBA), in 2019 more than 60 million people were employed at companies considered to be small businesses. That number translated to 47.1% of the private workforce. Note that 99.9% of all businesses in the United States are small businesses, which translated to about 31.7 million in that year. In addition, the SBA states that 5.2 million minorities are self-employed.[14] The fact that the United States has an agency dedicated to small businesses is an indicator of how important this social contract is to society.

The social contract, in this context, states that those who successfully navigate the daunting circumstances necessary to become an entrepreneur should expect to see their fortunes increase. As mentioned in the previous chapter, the social contract is good for society, along with the individual. In 2019, 1.6 net jobs were created by small businesses.[15] *Net* means that more were created than lost. It is a part of the American mythos that anyone from anywhere occupying any rung of the economic and social ladder can be successful. The stories of success fill the business pages but also creep into all areas of American society and culture. Companies that are household words, like Apple, Hewlett-Packard, and Google, were all started in garages by people with vision and the determination to be successful.[16] Company successes like these are why the lexicon has phrases such as "only in America" or "an American success story."

For a social contract to deliver on its promises to the citizens, there has to be some level of trust that engaging in the activities will produce the desired outcomes of upward mobility, both socially and economically. But upward mobility is not a given with entrepreneur-ship. Take, for instance, the problem of access to credit markets. No fledgling enterprise is successful without access to what economists would call *capital*, or in other words, enough working cash flow to endure the ebbs and flows of commerce.

An example might be an entrepreneur who starts a business mak-ing handmade Christmas ornaments. Clearly the holiday period, starting in late September and ending sometime in January, will be the peak earnings time. However, decisions about materials and inventories must be made well in advance. Those materials will need to be purchased long before any sales revenues are realized. The busi-ness owner must be careful not to overextend her resources, given that even though raw materials need to be purchased in advance, there are day-to-day expenses, like rent, that need to be paid regu-larly, regardless of sales. Economists normally refer to these as *fixed costs*, given that these expenses do not change regardless of circum-stances or the number of items or services sold. A business owner cannot simply skip paying rent to purchase materials.

This is where access to credit markets would be most beneficial. With access to working capital, the owner would be able to make payroll and pay rent while producing a stockpile of goods to be sold later. This is where the social contract runs into trouble. There are clear disparities in who has access to credit. As pointed out by Surekha Carpenter, "In many areas, the inability to secure an auto loan—and thus, a car—could limit employment options."[17] Without proper access to credit, entrepreneurs are left to seek alternative sources of funding, such as payday lenders. In such cases, individuals end up with more debt at the end of the venture than when they began, and that is clearly the sign of a less-than-ideal social contract. Access to credit should be uniform for citizens willing to engage in the activity. As discussed in Chapter 1, if the social contract is not open to all, that should be stated clearly. But is it really a social con-tract then? Maybe instead of a social contract, it could be called a "some of us in society contract."

Carpenter notes, "Minority borrowers, low-income borrowers, and borrowers in rural places face higher rates of denials for mortgages and small businesses."[18] This seems to run counter to the notion of what a social contract is designed to do. Minorities occupy strata on the income scale significantly lower than the rest of the country in the United States, and low-income borrowers are the ones most encouraged to engage in the social contract activities as a path to prosperity that does not require outsized charity. More to the point, it was stated in a 2019 test conducted by the National Community Reinvestment Coalition that "better-qualified Black and Hispanic small-business owners had worse experiences than their White counterparts when seeking business loans."[19] The lending gap during the COVID-19 pandemic only brought this failing of the entrepreneur social contract to the surface. In a recent National Bureau of Economic Research working paper, the authors stated the following concerning the Paycheck Protection Program (PPP):

> The original legislation authorizing the PPP included an explicit mandate to prioritize socioeconomically disadvantaged businesses. Yet, in practice, many conventional banks did not serve Black-owned firms in proportion to their share in the PPP borrower population. Instead, it was fintech lenders that made a disproportionate share of loans to Black-owned firms, accounting for over half of the PPP loans to Black-owned businesses. Among conventional lenders, small banks had a particularly low rate of lending to Black-owned firms. Why would this have occurred, given that PPP loans were 100% guaranteed by the federal government?[20]

In addition, there should be some care taken when thinking of entrepreneurship as it relates to the promise of upward mobility. The question put forth in a 2014 Urban Institute paper was rather simple: "Do higher-than-average incomes actually lead entrepreneurs to experience greater economic advancement relative to paid workers?" This particular social contract action was supposed to lead to higher economic and social standing due to the action taken. This was supposed to be the genesis of why society so firmly pushed individuals toward such actions. The findings by the authors were mixed. They stated, "We find no evidence in support of self-employment providing an advantage in achieving upward mobility. In comparison to wage-and-salary workers, the self-employed are far more likely to experience downward income mobility. Self-employment both significantly lowers the probability of upward mobility and significantly increases the probability of downward mobility in comparison to paid work."[21]

The probability of downward mobility has to be accounted for with the risk of failure of the enterprise. In other words, failure has a real risk of dropping people lower on the economic and social ladder than where they started, and the upside gain might not be as great as the contract promised. This clearly sounds like a lottery. What should not be minimized is that there is a great deal of risk associated with these endeavors. According to statistics from the Bureau of Labor Statistics' Business Employment Dynamics, 20% of small businesses fail in the first year and 50% fail by the fifth year.[22] Once again, the practice of the entrepreneur social contract does not match the theorized outcome, and society might want to consider adjustments before making iron-clad guarantees about the outcomes and judging people accordingly.

MILITARY SERVICE

Thinking of military service as a social contract does make sense, but maybe not in terms of how I have defined a social contract thus far. It is true that veterans are given a great amount of respect and admiration in the United States. There is a national holiday for veterans. There are preferential hiring practices at many companies for those who have served in the armed forces, and retailers, from large corporate entities like Home Depot and Lowe's, down to mom-and-pop restaurants, offer discounts on goods and services sold to veterans. This action of military service is clearly endorsed by society.

It is not too much of a stretch to see how military service might lead to higher standing on the economic and social ladder. The military touts itself as an institution where young people who have no experience in handling large-scale logistics or working with high-tech equipment can be trained to be experts in many fields, from communications to counterterrorism to food services and many others. The military also stresses the discipline needed to be a member of all branches of the armed forces and that entry is restricted to only those who are fit and prepared to endure months of grueling initiation to become a member. This type of grittiness and determination would conceivably make these individuals ideal candidates for later civilian employment. That experience alone should elevate veterans' earnings potential.

In this chapter, I have mentioned other society-endorsed activities, and the military is a way to have access to many of them, which should help individuals move up the economic and social ladder. Employers do not have to invest in extensive training, which can be expensive, and can readily hire experienced workers. Another benefit open to those who have served in the armed forces is the opportunity to gain a free or greatly reduced-cost college education. As mentioned earlier, receiving an associate's degree or higher puts households in the top half of all income earners. This benefit, in and of itself, seems to make military service an excellent activity for a social contract. In addition, veterans have access to health care through Veterans Administration (VA) hospitals. Given the rising cost of health care, having access to free medical care should greatly enhance veterans' ability to rise up the economic ladder and should be a stopgap against enormous unexpected medical expenses. I have discussed the theory and practice of entrepreneurship and the difficulties with attaining access to credit. Veterans can get home and business loans that are backed by the VA. More detail on this point will come later in the book. If it is true that access to credit is necessary for establishing successful small businesses, then having a good credit score through home ownership shows the benefit that military service can provide in facilitating that goal.

How we arrived at this point, where a veteran's status comes with so many benefits, requires some back story. After World War I, the United States had a difficult time reassimilating returning veterans, who struggled to find employment. This was true even with the aid of several government programs. Congress stepped up in 1924 to create the Bonus Act, which promised veterans a bonus for every day of service. The drawback was that the legislation stated that the bonuses would not be paid until 1945, which did little to help returning service members, given that 20 years was a long time to wait.[23]

In 1932, during the Great Depression, there was a march on Washington where 20,000 veterans protested, demanding their bonus money. They would clearly become an example of undeserving individuals protesting a social contract that did not live up to its promises. The government did not respond to the protest by admitting a mistake had been made. In fact, in an ironic twist, President Herbert Hoover sent the army to remove the protesting veterans.

Those first protesting veterans did not receive an early bonus, but they did lay the groundwork in the minds of government officials that something should be done to ensure the mistakes of the past did not occur again after World War II regarding veterans. In 1944, Congress passed and the president signed the GI Bill. Even though the bill is best known for the access it provided to educational opportunities, it did a great deal more. It provided a cost-of-living stipend and allowed those who wanted it an opportunity to continue their education, up to $500. The offer was taken up by many. In fact, in 1947, nearly half the admissions to college were veterans. Besides getting job counseling, veterans looking for work were given $20 in weekly unemployment benefits for one year. As mentioned before, there was also access to credit, which allowed for the purchase of homes, farms, or businesses. The promise to veterans was more fully embraced by society, and by 1956, nearly 10 million veterans had received GI benefits.

Since 1984, the GI Bill has been made permanent and is still used by veterans today. In 2008, Congress passed an amended version of the 1984 GI Bill called the Post-9/11 GI Bill, or Post-9/11 Veterans Educational Assistance Act. It stated that veterans on active duty on September 11, 2001, or after were allowed access to greater educational benefits. It also allowed veterans to transfer unused educational benefits to their spouse or children.[24]

Joining the military also provides a path to naturalization and obtaining legal status, which opens up a list of possibilities that would be limited or nonexistent for noncitizens.[25] What is appealing for individuals seeking to use the military as a path to naturalization is that some of the standard requirements for naturalization are waived. For instance, if an individual serves in the military during a period of designated hostilities, the requirement that the person reside in or be physically present in the US for any length of time before applying for naturalization can be waived. The length of time required is not too onerous for individuals seeking naturalization through military service, at just one year at any time, although finding enlistments of one year is virtually impossible. The "any time" phrase is interesting, given that people could have been in the military earlier in life, then later sought to apply for naturalization, since there is no statute of limitations on applying.

In practice, military service as a social contract has problems. Take, for instance, the notion that having served in the military means that veterans are automatically allowed to use GI Bill benefits to pursue educational goals. That was not entirely true during my time in the army between 1986 and 1989, nor is it correct now. What my recruiter failed to tell me was that simply signing up for the Army College Fund was not enough. If I really wanted to get funds for college later, I would need to have $100 deducted from my pay every month for the first year I was in the army. This was a sizeable outlay for me then, given that I would have to give up 25% of my pay. As a new recruit in 1986, I was paid approximately $400 per month. In 2023, a new recruit in the army is paid a bit over $1,900 per month, but the $100 buy-in requirement remains. The math is still pretty simple, in that a sacrifice of $1,200 provides access to enough money to pay for college later.[26] The fact that many recruits are unaware of this expense at the time of enlistment is troubling.

Some of my peers signed up, but after a few months they quit the program. Some were sending money back home or had families off base to support. The army was more than happy to refund all the money they had deposited. Why? Once a person dropped out of the program, they were not eligible for those college funds again during that enlistment. It is not automatic that being honorably discharged from the military means access to college funds.

Individuals are also surprised to find out that the VA is not actually in the college tuition business. During my college years, the VA required a monthly verification process to ensure I was still in good standing as a college student. After this monthly verification process was completed, I would receive a check. The complication faced by many students is that most colleges and universities have a three-week period at the beginning of each semester when tuition bills must be paid in full. It is difficult receiving monthly payments from the VA when school fees and other payments are due as a lump sum and immediately. It is especially confusing for low-income and first-generation veterans who are unfamiliar with the process of attending college. Of course, most campuses have offices designed to help veterans make the adjustment to becoming students.

The military as a social contract is close to matching theory to practice but is not perfectly aligned. Individuals should be made aware of that fact by society.

The aim of this chapter was to give context to what is meant by a society-endorsed activity that should lead to upward mobility on the economic and social ladder. I could have listed many other activities, and I am sure the reader is thinking of some now. Although the activities seem rather straightforward, it is not clear that they live up to their stated goals. What the coming chapters will do is provide case studies of when a group of individuals reached a tipping point about society-endorsed activities that did not provide promised results and how resulting protests developed.

4 Occupy Wall Street

Let us pretend that you, the reader, want to buy a house and I am a lender who wants to help with this financial transaction. Typically, the first thing I would do is run a credit check on you to ensure I can reasonably expect to be repaid the money I am going to put up to allow you to buy this house. I need to be sure you will be able to pay back the principal portion of the loan and some amount of interest that I will charge you. After all, the house is not really yours until you pay me back. However, I will forgo the normal checks that should be done. We will call this a *low doc*, meaning low documentation, or *no doc*, meaning no documentation, loan.

Another thing I will forgo is the requirement of "skin in the game," where I require that you have saved up at least 20% of the purchase price of the home. It's risky for you and me to proceed this way, but it will definitely be for the best. Without a vested interest in retaining your savings, you might be more cavalier about repaying me. There are other fees that normally occur with a home purchase, such as attorney fees, some form of closing costs, an appraisal to be sure the house is worth the purchase price, and others. We will simply roll all those costs into the loan. I will give you a loan for anywhere between 105% and 115% of the purchase price. You do not need to have any money to participate in this transaction, and you will not need a high credit score, either, given that I do not plan to check carefully anyway.

Some might frown on this arrangement, but they are not thinking of all the good that will occur. Many parts of the economy will benefit from this arrangement and, in theory, everyone will be much better off in the end. Think about those in the home building business. This type of arrangement should create an increased demand for construction workers. In addition, the American dream is predicated on homeownership, which should lead to stable communities and stronger bonds between neighbors. Local governments should be happy with this arrangement also, given that property tax coffers should swell from all the new homeowners. The finance industry should be ecstatic, given the number of loans being written and all the interest revenue that will be generated. Someone will need to sell all these properties being bought and sold, so new jobs will be created in the real estate business. People can sell properties in their spare time to generate extra income. Buying and selling real estate will be the next big thing and many fortunes will be made.

You obviously will be very happy to have a new home and will go out to buy furnishings for your new domicile. You might decide not to move into this home, given how hot the real estate market is. You might decide to buy a second or a third property, in addition to this one, to speculate on. Why not, given that access to credit is fairly easy with me as your lender? All you need to do is find a property where the value is going up. Given how all this demand is being generated for homes, prices are rising all over, so finding a good deal on a speculative property will not be too difficult. You could buy the properties with the money you borrowed, but you never intend to move in. The price of the property will go up enough so you are able to pay me back what you borrowed, with a tidy little profit for yourself, before the first mortgage payment is due. I am very happy regardless, since I did not have to wait 30 years for you to pay me back in installments, which reduces the risk of default over such a long time span. All the parties mentioned are still happy, except maybe the home furnishing stores, since you never went shopping. Someone will eventually move in, so furnishings will be bought at some point, and maintenance will be needed on the home to keep it looking nice.

I mentioned that I would like to be repaid sooner rather than later, so I am happy you flipped that property, meaning you bought it and then immediately sold it without intending to live in it. Had you taken a longer time to repay me, I would not be too sad. I could take your loan and package it together with other loans and do a few things with them. I might use them as collateral. I could go to an investment bank to borrow more money so I could make even more loans. The investment bank will be glad to lend the money to me, given that they have the retirement savings of many of the largest pension funds from around the country and have to generate positive revenue streams for the millions of people who have put their money in these funds. They can check my books to see that I will have a steady stream of income for many years from these bundled mortgage loans. They should be satisfied with this and can charge me an interest rate on the borrowed money that ensures there are positive returns. I could also take those loans and basically sell them off. I do not want to wait for my money, so I could sell them for immediate cash. I might do this by selling my packaged loans to a much larger financial institution. They can wait out the long stream of payments better than I can. In essence, someone else will own the loan, but I might still service it for them and collect the monthly payments. This means you will not realize that the loan now belongs to an entirely unknown party, although I will send you a notice in the mail where this minor detail will be hidden in the fine print.

Now let us pretend I made this loan to you with a very high interest rate. After all, I have to make money out of this deal somehow. We really do not care what the interest rate is, since you do not intend to hold the loan long enough to pay it back with interest. What we might also do is make the interest rate variable, and we will stipulate that all you need to pay me in monthly installments is the interest. The loan balance will remain the same, but you do not care. You are holding this property only long enough to find someone willing to buy it for more than what you paid for it. If you bought the place for $50,000 and paid me interest on it for five years, you would still owe me $50,000. Basically, this interest-only loan has allowed you to rent the property. This is not uncommon in the finance world. When investors are "shorting" a stock, they borrow a stock to make a financial gain, then return the stock with a fee. This is what you will do with the property. You will hold it and pay me a fee of interest until you sell it for more, which will allow you to recoup the interest payment. If shorting happens in other parts of the economy, why should you not be allowed to do the same?

The group of investment bankers, insurance firms, real estate brokers, me, you, and many others might know that you do not have the capacity to pay this loan back. However, you do not care, since you are going to flip the property as long as the price keeps going up. I am not terribly concerned either, given that I will sell your loan to a secondary market. Should the secondary market be concerned? Not really. They will write out an insurance policy that will pay them in the event that you and your neighbors all default. The insurance companies can go to federal agencies to be made whole if things get really dire. Thinking about it, I should probably go to a bookie and make a bet at any odds that you are going to default. The bookie will not have the inside information that I do that you are wholly unqualified for this loan and will present me with odds. After all, if I was making these reckless loans to you and everyone in the financial system was aware of it, it might cause a great recession when this entire house of cards falls. No one would figure that all of us would be so reckless with the economic health of the country.

In the end, if things do go bad, the government will bail out all of us. If the government does not help all of us but instead picks winners and losers, then there might be some resentment. The resentment will only be intensified if those picked to be helped are the very ones who caused most of the damage—for example, people like me. Those people not helped by the government might feel they are undeserving of their plight, and protest.

The scenario I just laid out is fictitious, of course, but borne out of fact. In 2007, the United States was at the beginning of the worst financial crisis since the Great Depression in the 1920s. It only got worse in 2008, when several of the largest financial firms failed, like Countrywide Financial, Bear Stearns, IndyMac, and Fannie Mae and Freddie Mac. The situation reached an apex on September 15, 2008, when the very large investment firm Lehman Brothers filed for bankruptcy.[1] The fear was that other investment banks would follow and there would be a collapse of the entire financial sector. This contagion would destroy the economy by making it impossible to get mortgage, auto, student, and business loans. In essence, all lending and borrowing would freeze up. With no lending or borrowing happening, commerce would be only a fraction of what it should and could be, and the resulting loss in economic growth would devastate the country.

In 2007, efforts by several government departments to stave off the coming financial crisis had begun—namely, by the Treasury Department, the Federal Reserve, the Federal Deposit Insurance Corporation (FDIC), and a few others. However, those efforts were not enough, given the size of the problem. Terms like "too big to fail" started popping up in the popular press. In late 2008, the Bush administration proposed the Emergency Economic Stability Act of 2008 (EESA). EESA had bipartisan support in Congress and was enacted on October 3, 2008. Congress authorized $700 billion for use to stem the tide. The act itself had many components, but the most memorable part was the Troubled Asset Relief Program (TARP). Officially, the government stated that the purpose of TARP was "to restore the nation's financial stability and restart economic growth." The Treasury stated, "While Congress authorized $700 billion for TARP, Treasury utilized far less than that. The TARP actual lifetime cost was approximately $31.1 billion, most of which was attributable to the program's efforts to help struggling homeowners avoid foreclosure."[2]

TARP was a massive undertaking by the government, given that the nation was losing almost 800,000 jobs per month and household wealth had fallen by 17%, which was a decline five times greater than what was seen in 1929, when the Great Depression began.[3] Things were looking very grim for the US economy. The stock market had dropped 500 points the day after Lehman Brothers fell. The problem was that borrowing and lending had ground to a halt. From my narrative earlier, those packages of bad, or "troubled," mortgages were causing massive defaults by the homeowners who could not pay the mortgage on a home they never intended to own. In addition, homeowners who genuinely wanted to own and maintain their property were faced with the very unpleasant prospect of paying a mortgage for a home that was not worth the value of the resale price. The terms heard were that they were "upside down" or "underwater," meaning they owned a home for which, if they tried to sell it, the value would be less than the loan. For example, paying $200,000 for a home with a resale value of $150,000 left many individuals with no other option but to file for bankruptcy. Many people simply walked away from their homes and left them for the banks to handle. The keys would be left on the kitchen counter, since continuing to pay made little sense. These types of actions ruined the credit of the homeowner and caused untold harm to local communities and families.

In 2009, then-President Obama urged Congress to pass the American Recovery and Reinvestment Act (ARRA), which they did. The act could have been known as TARP Part 2, although its stated goal was "to help create and save jobs, spur economic activity and invest in long-term growth." The question is whether all these efforts worked. That depends on who you ask. According to the Treasury Department, the answer was yes. They stated, "By the middle of 2009,

the government's coordinated response to the financial crisis had sta-
bilized the financial system and resulted in significantly lower borrowing rates for businesses, individuals, and state and local governments.
Companies were able to fund themselves in private markets by issuing
equity and long term debt. The value of the savings of Americans had
begun to recover. And the U.S. economy began to grow."[4]

However, there were many moving parts and many programs set
up as part of this coordinated effort. One part of the government
response that caught the attention of the general public, despite the
dizzying array of initiatives being rolled out simultaneously, was the
staggering amount of bonus monies being paid to top executives at
the very firms receiving government TARP funds. President Obama
expressed outrage that in 2008 a whopping $18.4 billion was paid
out in bonuses.[5] Wall Street argued that paying bonuses was a standard part of the historical payment structure for top executives. They
argued that top talent costs and that the country would be in terrible
disarray if people not versed in high finance were allowed to take the
reins of the economy.

A *special master* was authorized to address the public outcry
resulting from this situation. President Obama announced a cap of
$500,000 in annual salary at companies deemed to have had "excep-
tional assistance" under TARP. Even with this cap, half a million dollars in annual salary was several multiples of the average annual
salary in America. It was an even more staggering amount given that
annual salaries were falling, and many individuals had no salaries
because they had lost their jobs. Kenneth Fienberg was the first special master and was succeeded by Patricia Geoghegan.

In the report from the Deputy Special Inspector General for the
Troubled Asset Relief Program, which was written in January of
2012 and submitted to the Assistant Secretary for Financial Stability
at the Treasury, two sections stood out. The first section was the
identification of the companies that would be subject to oversight
regarding compensation, as well as which employees would need to

have their salaries regulated, and how. The section also laid out why things were occurring in the fashion that they were. There were over 700 financial institutions in the Capital Purchase Program, but the report listed seven as having received assistance that was deemed "exceptional." Many of them were household names and included American International Group, Inc. (AIG), Bank of America Corporation (Bank of America), Citigroup Inc. (Citigroup), Chrysler Financial Services Americas LLC (Chrysler Financial), Chrysler Holding LLC (Chrysler), General Motors Corporation (GM), and Ally Financial Inc. (Ally), formerly GMAC, Inc.

A limiting factor for the special master was that they could set the pay only for the 25 most highly paid employees at these firms. They could approve the compensation structures for the next 75 highest paid employees, but not the individual pay. The Treasury had six guiding principles for the special master. They included that the firms should avoid incentives that would take on risks, they needed to remain competitive and work to retain and recruit employees so the firms would be successful in repaying TARP, pay should be based on performance metrics, and pay should be consistent with that at similarly situated peer institutions.[6]

The reasoning in the first section of the report seemed sound and was designed to return stability to the financial sector. The second, more interesting section of the report recorded how things actually went. The report stated,

> SIGTARP found that the Special Master could not effectively rein in excessive compensation at the seven companies because he was under the constraint that his most important goal was to get the companies to repay TARP. Although generally he limited cash compensation and made some reductions in pay, the Special Master still approved total compensation packages in the millions. Special Master Feinberg said that the companies pressured him to let the companies pay executives enough to keep them from quitting, and that Treasury officials pressured him to let the companies pay executives enough to keep the companies competitive and on track to repay TARP funds. Given

OSM's overriding goal, the seven companies had significant leverage over OSM by proposing and negotiating for excessive pay packages based on historical pay, warning Special Master Feinberg that if he did not provide competitive pay packages, top officials would leave and go elsewhere.[7]

In essence, the operation failed despite its good intentions. The issue was that many people in the US saw all of this unfolding and were genuinely upset. It has been estimated that over 3.8 million homes were foreclosed on and the livelihoods of millions of people were destroyed as a result of this crisis, yet billions of dollars went to those people who, some would argue, had caused the problems. It seemed terribly unfair that these bonuses were being paid when so many were suffering across the country.[8]

Although it would be inaccurate to say that the executive compensation disaster directly led to Occupy Wall Street (OWS), the two have definite connections. In June of 2011, a phone conversation between Kalle Lasn and Micah White was the genesis of OWS. Both of them worked at a Canadian anti-consumerist magazine called *Adbusters*, where Lasn was the founder and White was an editor. On June 9, 2011, *Adbusters* registered the domain name OccupyWallStreet.org. Later, the team at the magazine would design a poster for their proposed protest and write out a tactical briefing.[9]

By this point, the group had designated September 17, 2011, as the day for the protest, which was to take place in New York City. The idea for the protest grew as word spread through social media, given that an account had been set up on Twitter with the handle @OccupyWallStNYC. In July there was a call from *Adbusters* for "20,000 people [to] flood into lower Manhattan, set up tents, kitchens, peaceful barricades, and occupy Wall Street for a few months."[10]

As planned, the protest did begin on September 17, with about 1,000 people gathering on the streets of Lower Manhattan and walking up and down Wall Street. Eventually, the protesters made their way to Zuccotti Park, which is about two blocks north of Wall Street. The protests garnered media attention and even more so over the coming weeks when celebrities like Rosanne Barr and Susan Sarandon showed up in solidarity. Academic Cornel West also lent support and filmmaker Michael Moore addressed the crowd of protesters, who had taken up something approaching permanent residence in the park.

Given the nature of the protests, it was not surprising that they were supported by the Transport Workers Union Local 100, which was the first large union to endorse the protest efforts through a member vote. The protests then began to spread across the United States, with OWS-inspired protests occurring in large metropolitan cities like Boston; Minneapolis; Washington, DC; and Los Angeles, and small communities like Portland, Maine; Memphis; and Milwaukee. In all, there were dozens of protests across the country, and even protests across the globe.

Out of these protests came the now-familiar refrains "Our finances are weak, but our spirit is strong. We are the 99 percent. Our spring is coming!" and "Banks got bailed out, we got sold out." Part of this resentment resided in the fact that most big banks survived the financial crisis mostly unscathed and, as mentioned previously, executive compensation was mostly unaffected. The protesters did not specifically name executive compensation as one of their grievances, but it was never far from the surface. As I discussed in Chapters 1 and 2, the United States has a long history of exaggerated income inequality. In fact, among the Organization for Economic Co-operation and Development (OECD) countries, the US was the only country during the 1980s and 1990s to experience an increase in prefiscal income inequality and yet engaged in less redistribution.[11]

The numbers relating to growth bear out the reasons for concern. Think of running a foot race. The race begins and one person jets out front. She is clearly a better conditioned athlete and takes a commanding lead. Even if she maintains a steady pace with no injections of speed, the gap between her and the others will grow. Now imagine that at times the other runners are fortunate to find themselves running downhill. As a result, they may be able to close the gap a bit

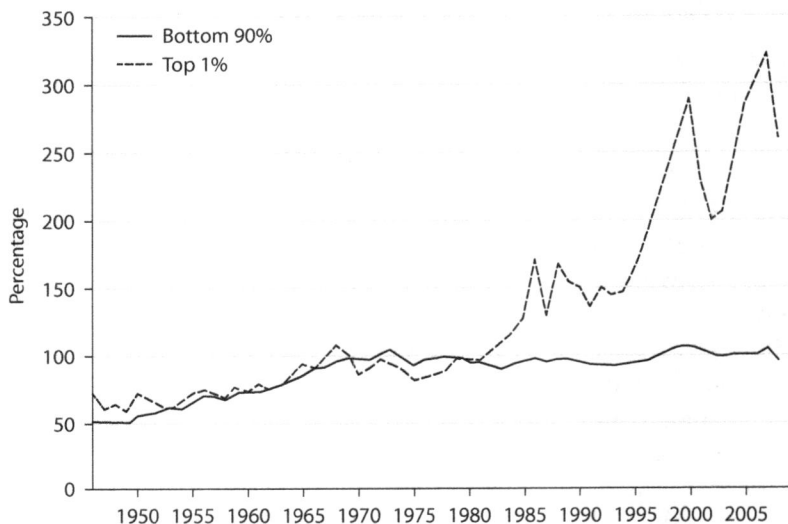

Figure 6. Average income between 1946 and 2008, as a percentage of the 1979 level. *Source:* Shaw and Stone, *Tax Data Show Richest 1 Percent Took a Hit in 2008*, fig. 3, citing Center on Budget and Policy Priorities calculations based on Piketty and Saez.

without ever coming close to overtaking the leader. There will be periods where their rate of gain, or rather pace, will surpass that of the leader. Now imagine that the leader decides to inject an increased pace of her own and speeds on to victory. The margin of victory will be much wider and leave the other runners so far behind they could be left to wonder if they were competing in the same race or if there were advantages available to the winner that they were not made aware of.

Let us examine Figure 6. There are two groups highlighted for the United States, starting right after World War II. One group are income earners in the top 1% of all earners, and the other group are the bottom 90% of income earners. The authors use 1979 as their basis year. In other words, the two groups have the same income in 1979 and both groups are at 100%. This makes comparing any other year and the difference between the two groups rather easy. If we look at the period before 1979, both groups are tracking pretty much the same. In fact, there are brief periods when the bottom 90% group is doing better than the 1% group. That all changes after 1979, when the 1% group takes off and never looks back. The authors state, "The average pre-tax income for the bottom 90 percent of households is almost $900 below what it was in 1979, while the average pre-tax income for the top 1 percent is over $700,000 above its 1979 level."[12] Those are both rather amazing stats. Those people in the bottom 90% group have incomes on par with those of people in 1979, and those in the top 1% of income earners are nowhere near the others and nearly a quarter of a million pretax dollars higher than where they were in 1979. Were these two groups in the same race?

As I have stated throughout this book, there does not need to be much concern from society about those at the bottom of the income distribution or in poverty if there is a system. The social contract assures these individuals that if they only would engage in certain activities, they too could rise above their circumstances. The fact that OWS started out rather small reflects this overarching belief among many about the strength of the social contract, and this may be the reason that such social movements do not take root often. As economists Dube and Kaplan point out, "Greater inequality may reflect as well as exacerbate factors that make it relatively more difficult for lower-income individuals to mobilize on behalf of their interests."[13] When individuals are engaging in the activities that should be assuring them upward mobility, it is very difficult to think about any type of injustices within the system. In essence, maintaining a lifestyle and providing for the family becomes the all-consuming goal. In such a case, it is not surprising that it took a while for OWS to resonate with more people.

The arguments of why these people were protesting were many, but they encapsulated the idea of being part of the undeserving. These individuals found themselves on the lower end of the social mobility ladder due to no fault of their own and wanted to voice their displeasure with how things turned out. If engaging in activities like education and healthy living were supposed to be the keys to getting ahead, how was it possible that some were getting ahead while others regressed? Had winners and losers been picked without regard to the social contract and its prescribed strictures?

The fact that it took the massive loss of well-being for millions, brought on by the financial crisis, only shows the power of the social contract in society and its staying power in influencing how we think about what causes mobility. Dube and Kaplan state, "A belief that we have a well-functioning electoral process dulls the incentives for independent social movement activism."[14] If I were to reword this sentiment, I would argue that a belief in a well-functioning social contract dulls incentives for independent movements. Those at the top of the economic and social ladder have little patience to hear the complaints of those at the bottom, given the social contract, and those at the bottom simply wait until the social contract works for them, because they have full faith in what they believe and hear, so there is little momentum for collective action. I agree with the authors' statement that "only after it became increasingly clear that the political process was unable to enact serious reforms to address the causes or consequences of the economic crisis did we see the emergence of the OWS movement."[15] However, I would change the words "political process" to "social contract." It does not happen often, but on occasion the undeserving do take notice and take action to be heard by the wider society.

The social contract would have its citizens believe in the value of hard work and industry as a means to achieve social and economic mobility. There is a saying that all work is honorable. However, it is not clear that all work leads to being among the highest on the income scale. For instance, as Dube and Kaplan note, "The biggest driver of upper-tail inequality—both in terms of capital and wage based income—was finance, the sector which governs the allocation of capital. Between 2002 and 2007, 34 percent of all private sector profits came from the financial sector."[16] The problem with what came out of the financial crisis was that finance was the very sector that made so many individuals wealthy but also the sector that caused harm for so many not remotely associated with financial markets. The social contract did not have a caveat that stated that if one engaged in the activities of the social contract, the gains made could be lost due to actors in a market far removed from the daily lives of most. It also did not state that some sectors of the economy were better than others regarding retaining gains made through hard work.

OWS did not last long. It was relevant for only about 60 days. It was a case of those who felt they were undeserving of their position on the economic and social ladder standing up and protesting their circumstances. Part of the publicity that OWS received was due to the drama involved when police pepper-sprayed female protesters. The scrutiny only intensified when police began to arrest protesters. Over 700 people were arrested, which occurred right before the eyes of the viewing public through television coverage and social media.[17] I would argue the reason this movement mattered in society was that the message, which was too muddled, resounded with many about what really counted for economic mobility and how it differed from what they had been told. As I wrote in Chapter 1, maybe the broader society and the protestors had different definitions of what the action required was supposed to be.

The failing of the OWS movement was that it did not have a clear objective and was decentralized on purpose. Goals were never clearly articulated despite there being a collaboration of many disparate voices, all expressing outrage with outcomes inconsistent with the social contract. For them to say the richest 1% of income earners had great influence on American government and business is a true statement, but what steps can a society take to rectify the situation? The argument that the system, or social contract, as I refer to it, does not operate as designed only works if a movement can first capture the attention of society as a whole and then engage society in a conversation about how to fix it. OWS succeeded with the first part but failed with the second. Some in society saw this movement as a call for a full-scale dismantling of American society and culture. It was dismissed out of hand as wanting to destroy American culture and replace it with some form of socialist propaganda.

In addition, OWS failed to be a movement for all those in the lower 99%. One of the great tragedies of the movement was its lack of resonance with the black community. With the fictitious story I laid out at the beginning of this chapter, I hoped to convey that some people with good intentions of paying for their homes were ensnared by what we now call "predatory lenders." Even though the story was set up with those who knew they could not pay for their homes willingly participating in a charade, there were millions of people who had very little interaction with credit markets or were first-time homeowners who were led to believe they would be able to pay for their homes with massive balloon payments, which would ultimately leave them without the ability to pay. Unscrupulous lenders preyed upon these people and their communities. That happened disproportionately in the black community. The Pew Research Center reported that between 2005 and 2009, black households lost just over half their median net worth, and recall from Chapter 1 that this community was already starting at a point of wealth dramatically lower than that of their white peers.[18] The financial crisis was especially harmful in closing the gap in wealth disparities.

So, the question is, why were the OWS protests predominantly carried out by white individuals? Part of the problem was the messaging. Take this excerpt from an essay written by Kenyon Farrow:

> One of the first photos I saw from the Occupy Wall Street protests was of a white person carrying a flag that read "Debt = Slavery." White progressive media venues often compare corporate greed or exploitation to some form of modern-day slavery. But while carrying massive amounts of debt, whether in student loans, medical bills, or predatory balloon-payment mortgages is clearly a mark of a society that exploits poor and working-class people, it is not tantamount to chattel slavery.[19]

The messaging was off-putting to many who still had to deal with the vestiges of that cruel and inhumane system of slavery. Ultimately, the opportunity to connect with this community was there, but squandered. The social contract had not lived up to its promises for large swathes of society, but the messaging was incoherent and incomplete, and as a result some of the undeserving were willing to sit on the sidelines.

One of the original architects of OWS, Micah White, had this to say in his 2016 book *The End of Protest: A New Playbook for Revolution*: "An honest assessment reveals that Occupy Wall Street failed to live up to its revolutionary potential: We did not bring an end to the influence of money on democracy, overthrow the corporatocracy of the 1 percent or solve income inequality." He added, "[It was] a constructive failure because the movement revealed underlying flaws in dominant and still prevalent theories of how to achieve social change through collective action."[20]

OWS was a great example of the undeserving taking action but failing to change the culture of society because they fundamentally misunderstood the nature of the social contract, which states that the system is perfectly designed and that those dissatisfied with their present circumstances need only look inward to find success. This notion was perfectly captured by Herman Cain, a successful businessman and former Republican presidential candidate, who said, "Don't blame Wall Street, don't blame the big banks, if you don't have a job and you're not rich, blame yourself!"[21] Clearly, Cain saw those lower on the income ladder as fleas or somehow impacted by a pathology or culture of dependency.

For some at the top of the income ladder, it is as easy as that. They perceive that the social contract has worked for them and is readily available for all, and therefore the problem must be with the user. As I mentioned in Chapter 1, there is a serious flaw in that logic in a practical business sense, yet it persists. What the OWS protestors could have done was demonstrate how they had, indeed, followed the tenets of the social contract but had not received the promised outcomes. They should have also stated that what they wanted was a sharing of the wealth and not a taking of the same. By this I mean that telling the highest 1% of income earners to give up their holdings in some real way is never going to be a winning strategy. However, pointing out that trying to achieve what they have, through the social contract that they firmly believe in, has some hidden and unintended pitfalls that make it difficult, if not impossible, might have been received more favorably if they could have clearly shown where the fault lines existed.

One of the phrases heard during the OWS protests was "Eat the rich!" Although this phrase has been around for centuries, this type of rhetoric only reinforced the hard-line approach taken by Cain and people sympathetic to his view. What is often forgotten in movements like this is that all outcomes requiring interactions between groups need not be zero sum, whereby the only way to make one person better off is to make another person worse off by an equal amount. Think about sharing a pie. If you and I are dividing a pie and I ask for a bigger piece, by necessity, the portion given to you will be smaller by the amount that my piece is larger. A way to fix this is for you and me to work together to have a bigger pie. With a bigger pie, I do not have to ask for a bigger piece to end up having more pie. After all, an equal portion of the bigger pie still gives me more. The beauty of this idea is that you end up with more pie also. The question then becomes, how do we make a bigger pie? The answer could lie in fixing the obvious and inherent flaws in the social contract, which would then make more people more productive and allow us all to contribute more effectively in making bigger pies.

5 The Tea Party

As we saw in the last chapter, a certain part of the population reacted negatively to the aftermath of the Great Recession and the efforts made by the government to stabilize the economy, and the country in general. It would not be too much of a stretch to say the OWS movement was the direct result of those efforts by the government. The idea of bailouts for the financial sector was upsetting to those who felt it was those same financial sector leaders who had caused the problems to begin with. However, the OWS protests were not the only protests to arise during that time period. Another group, the Tea Party Movement (TPM), would also take form and flourish. The grievances of the TPM members were that they had seen violations of the social contract for years before the Great Recession, and it finally reached a tipping point with the financial crisis. To a great extent, the Tea Party still exists today, although it has been morphed and subsumed into the larger Republican Party, with echoes of their arguments still being heard in the Make America Great Again (MAGA) movement.

Some scholars have argued that if the OWS movement was the voice of frustration with economic and social disparities from those on the political left, then the TPM was those same frustrations voiced by those on the political right. I would argue that the TPM members looked at the social contract and saw themselves as being part of the undeserving. TPM members saw themselves as people who had adhered to the tenets of the social contract but found themselves on the outside and ignored. They felt that after they had engaged in what they perceived as society-endorsed activities, they were still not as high up the economic and social ladder as their efforts warranted. They felt that their efforts had been used to elevate others above them while they toiled on the periphery.

One of the points I will continue to stress in this book is that those who feel they have legitimately engaged in the actions required by the social contract feel themselves absolved of concern or compassion for others who have not yet done or will not do the same, and this is what makes those other people deserving of their fate. Any efforts taken by the government to redistribute resources to those who only need to follow the path laid out for them by the social contract will be met with vocal and strong opposition. The TPM members felt that enough and, in fact, too much had already been done to take corrective action to see a convergence of wealth and income for those lower on the economic and social ladder. In an earlier chapter, I mentioned several social contracts and showed how many of them had inherent design flaws. The TPM members were not swayed by arguments that required any distribution from them to others, despite these perceived flaws.

In addition to the absence of any sympathy that might have been felt for those deserving of their status, having adhered to the tenets of the social contract allowed the undeserving, or in this case TPM members, to have righteous anger at the coercive efforts of Big Brother, or the government, to take away resources that had been earned and then give them to others who had not earned them. The anger was targeted toward both the government and those who received the help and support of the government. The government was filled with elites who had not earned their way and were living mostly off the efforts of hardworking Americans who faithfully paid taxes and went to work every day. The recipients of government aid were lazy and not willing to do anything to pull themselves out of their current standing. In the eyes of TPM members, the deserving had become so dependent on government aid, they had lost the ability to take care of themselves. They were fleas. No group of zealots are more determined to see their message carried forward than those who believe they are on the side of right and their anger is moral, justified, and designed to restore order. Messages like "if you don't work, then you should not eat" resonated with this group of protesters. The famous economist Walter Williams said, "If one person has a right to something he did not earn, of necessity it requires that another person not have a right to something that he did earn."[1]

A common refrain heard from those whom I have characterized as undeserving is that they had no help at all in attaining their status and anything they have or have achieved has been obtained or done due to sheer will and individual determination, along with grit. This group would be insulted to know that the social contract was designed to help them, along with others, secure the resources they have. They have totally embodied the ideas of rugged individualism and self-determination. The notion that anything or anyone other than their own hard work had any bearing on their standing in life would be met with staunch resistance. It is in this context that one should view the birth of the TPM, which has become a legitimate social movement.

What these individuals, who view themselves as being undeserving of their fate because of their own actions, failed to see and still fail to see is that there could be both a system where efforts result in reward and their hard work helped place them at their current standing. They view the matter as an either-or proposition. Either the system helped them or they did it on their own. There is no room for the possibility of both occurring. In addition, some reject the social contract altogether and simply see that they did, indeed, work very hard and are undeserving of any efforts to correct design flaws in the social contract or society.

If no one or no system helped them achieve a thing in life, then they take great umbrage with the notion of help for others. If they can do it on their own, then so can the rest of society. For those TPM members willing to concede that the system of the social contract does help in achieving higher status on the economic and social ladder, they argue that following the steps laid out by the system is a means to success and not redistributive efforts. The thing to take away from the birth of this movement and their protests is that there was no room for any form of corrective action by the social contract, since individual effort was all that was ever needed to climb.

What was the event that made these Americans so angry that they formed such a formidable movement? In part it was health care reform. In 2010, the Patient Protection and Affordable Care Act, which has also been referred to as the Affordable Care Act (ACA), or "Obamacare," was signed into law. According to the information provided on the website of the U.S. Department of Health and Human Services, the three primary goals of the law were to make affordable health insurance available to more people, expand the program known as Medicaid to all adults who had income 138% above the federal poverty level (FPL), and support innovative medical care delivery methods so as to lower the costs of health care.[2] These all seem like rather noble goals. As discussed in previous chapters, unhealthy workers are not very productive and become a strain on employers and the entire economy.

In essence, the act was designed to help people get health insurance who might normally have gone without. This group would include those who had a preexisting health condition that would have made it impossible for them to get insurance, those who did not have employer-provided health insurance, and those for whom the cost of paying for health insurance would have been prohibitive due to their financial situation.[3]

The way the system worked was to provide subsidies to households between 100% and 400% of the FPL. The legislation created health insurance marketplaces where individuals were supposed to be able to shop around for a health plan that fit their needs. Some of the advantages of the ACA were that the coverages were comprehensive and included physicals, vaccinations, doctor's appointments, and emergency care. The plan also forbid companies from denying coverage or raising rates based on an individual's health. All the information was in one place—the market—so making comparisons was easy. An interesting part of the plan was that it had no coverage limits, so a health provider could not stop covering an individual as medical bills climbed. In addition, there were out-of-pocket maximums that, in theory, were supposed to stop medical horror stories, like the one from Chapter 3, from occurring. There were other benefits that arose from the creation of the plan as well. The downside to the legislation was that plans were generally more expensive than other types of coverages, which included those an individual could have obtained through an employer.[4] In addition, plan options were limited, especially in certain areas of the country. Furthermore, signing up could occur only during a certain time of the year, which was referred to as *open enrollment*. In this regard, some care and preplanning was needed. There were also other drawbacks associated with this massive endeavor.

But how was all of this to be paid for? The short answer was new taxes and penalties that would be paid by individuals and businesses. The initial estimates were that tax revenues would amount to approximately $514 billion by 2023.[5] In essence, the program was going to provide tax credits to low-income individuals and introduce higher tax rates for higher-income individuals. The cutoffs were to be $200,000 for individuals and $250,000 for households, meaning higher-income people would be taxed and lower-income individuals would receive the tax credits.[6] In addition, there was the *individual mandate*, which required most Americans to buy health insurance.[7]

The mandate was implemented to increase the size of the pool of participants in the insurance market. Health scholars, including health economists, have long known there is a correlation between health and income, meaning that, in general, health metrics rise as income does. This means that a relatively wealthier individual is healthier, which could result in lower insurance premiums, and because this person has a higher income, they also have the means to pay the premium. The situation is reversed for a lower-income individual, who could have a higher medical risk profile but limited means to pay a higher insurance premium. The premium would be higher because of their health profile, which is correlated with a lower income. Unfortunately, those most in need of medical insurance are those least likely to have it.

The individual mandate was supposed to help that situation by combining the relatively healthy and unhealthy. Obviously, the objection from the wealthy would be that they are being forced into an insurance pool they do not want to pay for. The objection would also come from the lower-income individual, who does not want to pay for insurance because the cost is so high. By pooling all people, the theory was that wealthier and healthier individuals would pay into a system they would rarely need the services of, and thus funds could be used to supplement the health needs of the less wealthy and healthy individuals who would use the system more often. Lower-income individuals would receive a subsidy to help them pay the insurance premium, and the premium itself could be lower because of the influx of so many new customers. To keep people from declining to enroll in the system, there were fines associated with a failure to participate. Beginning in 2014, the act required all Americans to obtain health insurance or pay a tax penalty that gradually increased to the greater of $695 per person or 2.5% of household income when it fully came into effect in 2016 (with some exceptions, such as if coverage was deemed unaffordable). The provision did not last and was repealed in 2019, when the penalty rate was reduced to $0.[8]

In total, there were about 21 tax policies that were connected to the ACA.[9] I will not detail them all, but some are worthy of mention. I will add that not all of these initiatives have survived. Initially, there was a 2.3% tax on medical device manufacturers, but that has since been repealed. Another initiative that ended up being repealed was the "Cadillac Tax," which was a 40% excise tax on high-end premium health insurance plans. The "Medicine Cabinet Tax" stated that if an adult American had a Health Savings Account (HSA) or a Flexible Savings Account (FSA), they could not use health-reimbursed pretax dollars to buy nonprescription drugs. However, this provision was repealed as part of the 2020 CARES Act. Now, certain over-the-counter medications and products, as well as menstrual care products, are eligible for HSA and FSA reimbursement without a prescription. The law also stated there would be caps, or limits, on the amounts that could be contributed to HSA and FSA accounts annually. That stipulation remains, but the limits are adjusted every year to account for inflation. There was a 10% tax on indoor tanning services. That one remains. An annual fee was initially charged to health insurance providers. The thinking was that these companies would benefit from the large influx of new customers who would be purchasing health insurance under the new law and be flush with extra cash revenues. The fee took effect in 2014 but was suspended twice, in 2017 and 2019. However, it continued to apply for the 2018 calendar year. Interestingly, it applied for the 2020 calendar year but was repealed in 2021. Clearly, there was a dizzying array of taxes and initiatives, all designed to bring health insurance to millions of people.

One of the oldest and most celebrated concepts in economics is that of the meeting point of supply curves and demand curves. This happy outcome is commonly referred to as the equilibrium point, where the quantity demanded of a good or service precisely matches the quantity supplied of the same good or service. For anyone who has studied economics at any level, from middle school to graduate school, this point is driven home: Individuals find their way to this equilibrium of quantity and price without any need for intervention by an outside party, like a government. The point is further driven home that outside interventions distort the market equilibrium. One such outside intervention is a tax. An interesting aside is that it does not matter whether the tax is levied on the buyer (consumer) or the seller (business).

When teaching this concept in my classes, I normally refer to two time periods and what they look like. There was the period in the market before the implementation of the tax and the time period after the tax. We then study what happened to the market environment in the two periods. Before a tax, the price that a buyer is willing and able to pay is exactly the same as the price at which the seller is willing to sell the product or service. In addition, the quantity the seller provides is exactly the same as the quantity the buyer receives. However, in the period after the tax, a few things have changed. The price that the seller receives for the product or service is no longer equal to the price that the buyer pays. The difference between the two prices is the amount of the tax. It is not a hard concept to grasp. When we go to a convenience store, most of us understand that the price we see marked on an item is a before-tax price, and thus when we arrive at the register to check out, we are anticipating a higher price that includes the tax.

Because the price is higher due to the tax, we buy less of the good or service than we might otherwise. The after-tax market environment has a price that differs for buyers and sellers and a quantity that is a bit less than before. Another change that has occurred is there is now an amount of revenue generated from the tax that the government can use to fund operations and initiatives. Another curious part of the after-tax market environment is an area that is not revenue to the government or a benefit to the consumer or seller. Economists refer to this as the *deadweight loss* of a tax, since it is an area where benefits were not transferred between buyers and sellers,

Figure 7. Graph showing how a tax creates a wedge between supply and demand where deadweight loss exists. *Source:* Created by author.

nor did a benefit go to the government in terms of tax revenue. It is benefit that has just disappeared and been lost to the market. Some have argued that this deadweight loss is yet another reason to object to taxes. The argument is that taxes are not efficient due to this dead-weight loss. However, the TPM never made these arguments in objecting to the taxes required to fund the ACA (Figure 7).

The origins of the modern TPM can be reasonably traced to a television personality named Rick Santelli, who was working as a commentator for CNBC in January of 2009.[10] There is some debate on this point, with scholars saying that the movement actually began well before then and that frustrations with economic outcomes started earlier with the Bush administration, but these ideas of vocal and sustained protests crystalized in the Obama years. As mentioned in the last chapter, many Americans were upset with the aftermath of the financial crisis and TARP efforts even before the ACA came into existence. Santelli, the TV personality, was speaking from the floor of the Chicago Mercantile Exchange about the mortgage relief efforts that were taking place and suggested there should be a Chicago Tea Party to protest government intervention in the housing market. Within weeks, chapters of the Tea Party were springing up around the nation. Just like the OWS movement, the TPM was not a singular body. As Eastland-Underwood states, "The TPM is diffuse and decentralized, with dozens of independent organizations across the United States and no clear hierarchy of leadership. No single individual or group holds ownership over the ideas, and so selecting a single ideological framework may not accurately represent the values of the whole."[11] There was no single leader speaking on behalf of the group, nor was there one central location to go to for information about the demands or grievances that were being voiced. In addition, like OWS, the TPM had slogans that stuck with people and to some extent expressed their frustrations in the acronym TEA: Taxed Enough Already.

Like OWS, social media helped with recruiting and turning the movement into a force that would become a social movement. I mentioned earlier that referring to the TPM members as undeserving poor would be inaccurate. After all, more than 37% of TPM members were college graduates. Another statistic was that approximately 40% were evangelical Christians.[12] President Obama was a great recruiting tool for the TPM. Membership swelled as unfounded rumors circulated on social media and some mainstream media outlets that Obama, who frequently discussed his Christianity publicly, was secretly a Muslim. There were many members who were drawn to the movement as "birthers"—individuals who did not believe Obama could legitimately be president, given that they believed he was not a United States citizen. This notion persisted even though the director of the Hawaii State Department of Health released a statement that said she had seen his birth certificate and could confirm that he had been born in the state. Social media was a great tool for spreading and growing such stories.[13]

The first set of major protests began on April 15, 2009, which is historically Tax Day in the United States. Obviously, this day was intentionally picked to signify that the group was dissatisfied with government taxing and spending, and the deficit financing required to achieve some stated goals, like providing for the ACA. Quoting from Eastland-Underwood, "In the paragraph dedicated to 'Constitutionally Limited Government', the TPP explains, 'Like the founders, we support states' rights for those powers not expressly stated in the Constitution'. The Constitution does not expressly delegate power of the management of health care to the federal government, or for that matter, any welfare programmes."[14]

The TPM flexed their might during the 2010 midterm elections, when Republicans picked up 60 seats in the House of Representatives, which gave them a majority, and narrowed the majority that Democrats held in the Senate. It would be inaccurate to say that TPM members were enthusiastic Republican supporters, but later Republicans would work hard to incorporate them and their message into their talking points. As Marcus Hawkins wrote, "The tea party does not exist to challenge only Democrats simply to return the same Republicans who rubber-stamped the big government Bush agenda for eight years. And this is why the first victims of the tea party in any given election cycle are always Republicans."[15] As a way to thwart an onslaught of primary campaigning, Republicans embraced the movement, and as a result the Republican Party saw many Tea Party candidates elected.[16]

It is a bit puzzling that the Tea Party Movement chose their name in reference to the Boston Tea Party of 1773. At the time of the Stamp Act of 1766, there was no United States of America, and the colonies of North America were still under British rule, which meant all the revered figures instigating a protest against taxes from the home country were British. The Stamp Act required that all printed materials—such as playing cards, leaflets, and legal documents—be printed on embossed (with a revenue stamp) paper. The law was very unpopular among the colonists, mainly because they felt they had not been consulted and their interests were not represented in Parliament. However, as Eastland-Underwood writes,

Edmund Burke explained this at the time when he said Parliament represented "one nation, with one interest, that of the whole, where not local purposes . . . ought to guide, but the general good." For the colonists, Parliament could not represent colonial interests because the members were too disconnected with the local experience of Americans. James Otis, often credited as the author of the phrase "taxation without representation", wrote that you could "as well prove that the British House of Commons in fact represent all the people of the globe as those in America." By contrast, all TPM activists had the right to vote for their representatives in the modern, American democratic system.[17]

The parallels between the Boston Tea Party and the TPM do not hold up, given that the elected officials in office when the ACA was passed represented all parts of the modern society and democracy. Sometimes people just want to be heard, even though the outcome does not change things. In 2008, I published a paper titled "Elected versus Appointed School District Officials: Is There a Difference in Student Outcomes?"[18] The research question was rather simple: Did students perform better when school officials, either the superintendent or the school board, were elected to their positions as opposed to appointed? The argument could be made that appointed officials, who were shielded by one layer of bureaucracy, might implement policies that helped student achievement but were unpopular with the voting public. The results of my research showed there were no significant differences in student achievement when officials were elected or appointed. This led me to question the reason for the two styles of management, given that students were not impacted regarding their test scores. What I realized was that elected officials made themselves more accessible to the public by holding more meetings that the public could attend, at various locations around the district and at times more amenable to public attendance. So even though there was no difference for their children, some parents felt better because they had been given the opportunity to provide their input. Being heard matters even when it does not have any material impact on the outcome. Maybe more input and consultation were needed for TPM members to feel heard, but given their fundamentally different view on the purpose and implementation of the social contract, it is doubtful.

To say there were many similarities between OWS and the TPM would be a stretch, even though both groups essentially viewed the excesses that led to the Great Recession and the remedies taken by the government to correct them as flawed. The groups themselves would say they had nothing in common with each other. Both groups were primarily composed of white individuals (though the OWS members tended to be much younger), so they did have that in common. What ultimately set the two groups apart was how they thought the implementation of a "true" social contract should be achieved.

Slogans for both movements were propelled by social media, which helped spread the messages and organizing around protesting efforts. As mentioned previously, "We are the 99%" became synonymous with OWS, while TPM had sayings like "Take back our country." The latter phrase carried the undercurrents of what would become MAGA in 2015. The same sentiments could still be heard in 2024 when Donald Trump ran for the presidency for a third time.

When the OWS movement began, right-wing pundits described the protesters as "deluded" and "dirty smelly hippies." The term used most often to describe OWS members was *anarchists*.[19] People who saw a system of economic growth that led to inequalities in income and wealth wanted to dismantle it and construct a new system, which would presumably be more equitable. These income, wealth, and health disparities defy the notion of a functioning social contract, and as such, these OWS individuals wanted to see the system changed, or at least modified. The TPM could also be described as anarchists, although they would vehemently oppose such a characterization. In 2013, a government shutdown was triggered by members of the House of Representatives who were Tea Party members.

TPM members saw government spending as being out of line with the ideas of fiscal conservatism, which called for less deficit financing and fewer redistributive policies. I would argue that inhibiting the government from performing its functions is a form of anarchy; even though the government still existed, it ceased to perform its elected functions. Also, there have been several occasions when the government has been brought to the brink of not raising its debt ceiling as a result of TPM efforts.[20] Through elected office, it appeared the TPM members were more effective in implementing their vision than OWS members.

The question remains regarding how the overall society viewed the two movements. In that regard, a survey done around the time of the movements showed that 39% of survey participants supported the OWS movement, while 35% opposed it. On the other hand, only 32% of survey participants supported the TPM, while 44% opposed it.[21] The two groups clearly were not viewed the same by the general public. In the same *Time* article that quoted the survey results, David S. Meyer, a political scientist at the University of California Irvine, was quoted as saying, "When mainstream media, politicians and people milling at the water cooler are talking about political and economic inequality, the Occupiers are winning."[22] I would not totally agree with that assessment. The Tea Party and its members are still faintly recognizable in Congress, and out of the TPM sprang the beginnings of the social movement that propelled Donald Trump to the White House in 2016 and then again in 2024. The remnants of the OWS movement might be said to exist in the popularity of political figures like Vermont Senator Bernie Sanders. My overall assessment is that the TPM won.

It also appeared that major media organizations paid attention to the TPM much earlier in its existence. There did not appear to be any violence associated with any of the TPM events, and that begs the question of whether the early confrontations with police actually helped propel the OWS movement into the national consciousness in a way the TPM never needed to be. Both groups were masterful in incorporating religious figures, entertainers, and politicians into their cause. Both had grievances with what I have termed the social contract and were able to rally support to their cause by articulating those grievances in a manner that appealed to millions of people in the population, although not the same millions.

When individuals who feel they are part of the undeserving, or outsiders, reach a tipping or inflection point, then protests will arise. In the case of the TPM, it was the aftermath of the financial crisis and the rollout of the ACA that caused them to swell in numbers behind a common theme. This statement might seem at odds with statements I made earlier in this chapter about there being no grand organizing mission or theme of the TPM, and more so, they were a loosely connected network of smaller groups. But I can state there was a uniting theme, whether the smaller components knew it or not. They felt they were the ones who were being targeted unjustly, despite the fact the ACA could have been beneficial for all. Members of the TPM felt there had been a distortion of the social contract, which they believed required definitive action by individuals, and then some benefits would follow. If benefits came from redistribution that did not require action, then they, TPM members, were actually the victims and had every right to protest and seek redress. After all, they had played by the rules and climbed or attempted to climb following the specified actions dictated by those higher up on the ladder. Why then should funds be redistributed to those who had not or would not attempt to do the same?

Part of the problem with the rollout of the ACA was that it failed to couch these changes as productivity-enhancing enactments of the social contract. As mentioned previously, the social contract as it relates to health care is crucial. Workers who are healthier are more productive. The ACA was always touted as humanitarian, in that it was the right of all humans to be healthy. It would probably have been more appealing to the masses and maybe even TPM members had it been stated that this was a preventive step, in that paying for health care earlier on would pay for itself many times over in increased gross domestic product (GDP), which would benefit the entire society in the future. In addition, the argument could have been made that by expending these tax funds in this manner, costs could be saved in other regards. For instance, a better approach would have been to talk about real savings in other areas, such as savings from fewer emergency room visits by lower-income individuals, which are much more expensive than regularly scheduled visits to a health care provider. No one in the administration spent any time telling the population where they could correspondingly expect to see taxes fall, if that was even possible. As I wrote before, the ACA was supposed to pay for itself, in essence, by way of fees, taxes, and an increased pool of individuals. Stating that taxes could potentially be decreased in the areas of transportation, energy expenditures, or some other metric would have appealed to the masses. It was an opportunity missed.

The ACA also was more about insurance than actual health care. The connection between the two is clear. Most individuals do not have enough cash reserves to go to a doctor and pay for services out of pocket, and it seems impractical to save for events that cannot be predicted. That is why insurance is a good alternative. As mentioned earlier in this chapter, insurance also allows for risk pooling, which theoretically lowers costs. However, economists and others have noticed a strange behavior that can take place when people have insurance, which they call *moral hazard*.

Imagine the following scenario: You go to rent a car and are asked if you want to spend a bit extra on the company insurance policy. With this policy in hand, you are covered against paying for any damages that might occur while the car is in your possession. Knowing this, you drive much more recklessly than you would otherwise. After all, you are not obligated to pay for any damages, no matter how expensive. Now, imagine the same scenario regarding health insurance. Knowing you are covered by an insurance policy, you might engage in more reckless behavior because you know if you are injured or fall ill, the costs of health care will be greatly reduced, or maybe even totally erased.

Since it is generally more cost-efficient to provide preventive health care and training as opposed to care after illness or injury, it might have been more effective to provide actual health care than insurance. In some regards, we saw this happen during the COVID-19 pandemic, when vaccines were provided at no cost to billions across the globe and to millions in the US, given that the cost from loss of life, lowered productivity, and suffering was much more expensive than the vaccine.

The next logical step, given what I have articulated thus far, would be to provide free health care to the population, but TPM members rejected this idea before it ever took form. Nationalized health care was seen as the antithesis of the social contract, where individual action was required for social and economic gain. The group made the claim that they stood for fiscal responsibility and free markets. As their Acadiana website states, "WE, the people, insist that our government return to the ideals of our Republic as set forth by our founding fathers with systems of Capitalism, Free Enterprise, and Free Will—NOT socialism, fascism, or nationalized bureaucracy." Even more directly from We the People of West Virginia, "NO TO SOCIALISM AND SOCIALIZED MEDICINE!"[23] If they opposed the ACA as socialized medicine, then the idea of providing health services for the entire country was a nonstarter for the group.

It is the theory of the social contract and individual action reaping reward that explains how we have the system we have in the United States. As Eastland-Underwood writes, "The American welfare system has long been considered an anomaly by comparison to other advanced democracies, and the lack of a public health care system is one of the prime examples."[24] Our US system of health care makes sense when couched in the context of our social contract. If an individual moves up the economic and social ladder due to their own industry and determination, then they will be able to access better options for health care, and these efforts do not require any charity or, in this case, government intervention. The TPM would stress that the efforts of the government should be to ensure that everyone has access to the economic and social ladder. If people choose not to climb, then they are deserving of their station and the subsequent health outcomes that come with it.

6 The Arab Spring

So far, we have looked at examples of people who have come to the conclusion they are undeserving of their station in life and on the economic ladder in the United States. But the world is full of social contracts. For example, China has pursued an aggressive strategy of annual growth with the promise that this strategy would be of benefit to all. However, the social contract might be critiqued if wealth inequality were to rise as a result and some were left too far behind. Or, in a more modern context, there could be psychological angst felt by Russian war veterans who return home from the war in Ukraine in search of promised services to help them reintegrate into society if they find that those promised services are not there or fall short of expectations.

The list could go on and on and each situation could be a chapter in itself. In the end, it does not matter what the social contract looks like. What matters is how long groups of citizens will allow obvious flaws in the execution of the social contract to exist, what mechanism or tipping point will cause them to protest, and how loud the voices of those who find themselves being, what I have termed, the undeserving will grow.

Thus far in this book, I have mostly refrained from judging which social contract is best for a society. That decision should be determined by the members of said society. I will, however, take great pains to point out deficiencies that exist in a social contract that prevent it from achieving its stated goals. In some cases, the social contract would never be able to achieve the stated goals, even if it were executed perfectly. More often than not, the problem is that citizens expect promises to be fulfilled from adherence to the tenets of the social contract, even if they are unrealistic. People expect to be rewarded for their behavior, even if the behavior does not warrant reward, because they have been indoctrinated to expect it.

I will begin this chapter by providing a brief history of how the Arab Spring unfolded to give context to the social contract that existed at the time. It is a very complicated and winding story, with entire books being written about the many-faceted political, economic, social, and religious factors that cause protests that sometimes turned deadly. I will give a rather simplified accounting of those events. The focus of this chapter is to delve into some of the economic factors that were implicit in the social contract and were critical to individuals' reaching their tipping point.

IRAN

For several reasons, as discussed below, it would be inaccurate to say Iran had protests that could be attributed to the Arab Spring uprisings. This might partly be explained by most of the region speaking Arabic, whereas Iranians speak Farsi. Thus, many Iranians would argue that they are not Arabic, so the term "Arab Spring" would not be appropriate to them. Regardless, some would argue that had the events of 2009 not taken place in Iran, the Arab Spring would not have happened in other countries later. The state had clamped down hard on the populous by the spring of 2011 because of these events, now known as the Green Movement. As Akbar recounts,

> Four candidates participated in the 2009 presidential election: the then president Mahmoud Ahmadinejad, Mohsen Rezaei, Mir Hossein Mousavi, and Mehdi Karoubi. All four candidates were approved by the Guardian Council, a non-elected government body. Each of the three candidates competing with Ahmadinejad had occupied significant positions in the Islamic Republic. Rezaei was a former head of the Iranian Revolutionary Guard Corps (irgc), Karoubi a former speaker of the parliament and Mousavi a former prime minister of the Islamic Republic. The latter two belonged to the reformist camp, and various thinkers, activists and scholars with reformist mindsets supported one of these two figures. Mousavi's popularity significantly increased when the former president of Iran Mohammad Khatami supported him after initially indicating that he would stand for the position again. Mousavi thus became the main reformist candidate in the presidential election.[1]

In June of 2009, the presidential election results were announced and Ahmadinejad was declared the winner. Mousavi and his supporters were skeptical and disappointed with the results. There was a peaceful protest in the capital city, Tehran, by supporters of Mousavi:

> From this point, what came to be known as the Green Movement began to take shape. The color green used in the election campaign remained the symbol of the movement. The Guardian Council decided to recount only 10 percent of the votes cast, and then declared that the election had been fair. Not unsurprisingly, this did not appease the protesters and the street demonstrations against Ahmadinejad's presidency continued for several months.[2]

There were no mass protests in Iran by the time of the Arab Spring uprisings in other countries, although Mousavi and Karoubi had called for them. The response of the government was to put the two under house arrest. The actions of the state were swift and brutal, with no meaningful reforms achieved, and "from this time onwards, supporters of reformist candidates have called for the release of Mousavi and Karoubi, but have failed to rally in the streets or organize significant demonstrations against the government—a further sign demonstrating that the movement has failed to survive."[3]

TUNISIA

With the events of Iran as a backdrop, I will begin in Tunisia. It can be argued that the boiling point for all the Arab Spring events was first reached in the middle of December 2010 when a Tunisian fruit vendor named Mohamed Bouazizi was told by local police that he would not be allowed to continue selling fruit from his small cart.[4] In protest, the jobless graduate set himself on fire and later died from his injuries. Around that same time, WikiLeaks released documents that showed the US government was critical of the government of President Zine El Abidine Ben Ali, who had ruled Tunisia for the previous 24 years. Young people protested in the streets over their general dissatisfaction with the economy and the circumstances that caused a poor street vendor to kill himself in protest over being willing and able to earn a living but not being allowed to do so.

After more than 10 days of vocal street protest, President Ben Ali appeared on television stating that government reforms would be enacted toward creating more jobs for the population. He also stated that protestors would be dealt with sternly. The protests continued despite the warnings from the president, and on January 11, 2011, 11 people died in clashes with police forces who violently tried to quash the protests, which had seen major demonstrations in several Tunisian cities, with cars being set on fire and other violent activities. The protests were successful, and on January 14, the president fled to Saudi Arabia. The prime minister, Mohamed Ghannouchi, then announced that an interim government would be formed after the abdication by the president. The unity government proposed by the prime minister would have included some of the members of the

previous government and that was deemed unacceptable by the protesters, who continued to march in the streets. By the end of February
2011, the prime minister himself resigned because the protests had
been going on continuously since the beginning of the year.

By the middle of March, the Tunisian supreme court ruled that
the party of President Ben Ali would be dissolved, which led to massive street celebrations by the citizenry. By the fall of 2011, the polls
opened for new elections in the country. On January 14, 2012, there
were massive celebrations marking the one-year anniversary of the
overthrow of Ben Ali.[5]

LIBYA

On the same day the president of Tunisia was fleeing the country, the
first reports of unrest were being heard in Libya. The leader of Libya,
Muammar Gaddafi, went on television to condemn the protests in
Tunisia. Only two days later, on January 16, 2011, human rights
activists were arrested in Benghazi, which set off protests there.
These protests were deadly, and by the middle of February there had
been a reported 230 deaths, with the numbers rising. The son of
Gaddafi went on television to defend his father and his actions. By
this point protests were occurring all across the Middle East and had
reached the Libyan capital city, Tripoli.

In the middle of March of that year, the United Nations backed a
plan to have a no-fly zone over Libyan airspace. The no-fly zone was
an attempt to keep the Gaddafi government from killing innocent
civilians in the chaos of the time. The United Nations had declared
that the violence constituted "crimes against humanity." The violent
response to protestors had captured the attention of the world, but
the leader, Gaddafi, opposed such an action by the UN and warned
that the imposition of the no-fly zone would be met with armed
resistance. There was an armed assault on the Libyan government
on March 19, when the US, France, and Britian agreed that NATO

should take military control of the no-fly zone. Military actions continued, and in the middle of April, then–US President Obama committed to the removal of Gaddafi as leader. Strikes and counterstrikes continued through the summer. At one point, the British embassy in Tripoli was set on fire in response to NATO air strikes. Other nations were targeted also. Even as late as September of 2011, Gaddafi was defiant and stated he would "never leave the land of his ancestors," in stark contrast to the situation in Tunisia, where President Ben Ali had been gone for over six months at that point. Gaddafi was defiant even after a mass grave with over 1,270 bodies was found in Tripoli. It would be a month later, in October, when Gaddafi was found and killed. Less than a month after the death of Gaddafi, his son, Saif, was arrested trying to flee to Niger. Just like in Tunisia, by the end of 2011 all remaining members of the previous government would be ousted from power. This was a rather dramatic event on the world stage, since Muammar Gaddafi had ruled the country for the past 42 years.[6]

EGYPT

The beginning of protests in Egypt mimicked those of Tunisia. In the middle of January 2011, a man set himself on fire next to the Parliament building in Cairo, the capital city, to protest economic conditions in the country. Less than a week later, coordinated protests began, with people demanding the ouster of President Hosni Mubarak, who had been in power for more than 24 years.

After only four days of protests there had been 24 deaths, which prompted Mubarak to make a televised announcement that he had dismissed his government. In addition, he pledged to pivot toward a more democratic form of governance but refused to step down as leader. The country's army soon declared it was aligned with the protestors, and the next day Mubarak announced he would not run for reelection; however, he would stay on to oversee the transfer of power. If things were not chaotic and violent enough, they got worse when individuals who were loyal to Mubarak took clubs, bats, and knives to Tahrir Square in Cairo to end the protests by attacking protestors. Within a week of that event, Mubarak officially resigned and handed power over to the military. The protestors seemed dissatisfied with this outcome, given that the military was not amenable to a quick transition to a civilian-led government.

Demonstrations continued, and by August of 2011, the military had brought in tanks to end the protest in Tahrir Square. The next month, the military announced there would be parliamentary elections, but the protestors feared the new government would be similar to that of the Mubarak-led regime. The situation continued to deteriorate when violence spread beyond Cairo and Alexandria. By the end of November of that year, the interim government that had been in place since Mubarak left bowed to public pressure and allowed the first free-ballot election in the country in over 80 years. The outcome of the vote saw large gains for the Muslim Brotherhood's Freedom and Justice Party. There needed to be a runoff election, but in December, Kamal Ganzouri, who was appointed prime minister by the military rulers, swore in a new government. In June of 2012, two important events took place, when Muslim Brotherhood-backed candidate Mohammed Morsi won Egypt's presidential runoff election and former President Mubarak was sentenced to life in prison by an Egyptian court.[7]

SYRIA

Protests arrived in Syria later than in the other countries mentioned. It was not until March of 2011, when a teenage boy was arrested in the city of Deraa for writing graffiti critical of President Bashar al-Assad, that demonstrations began. The rallies began in Damascus and Aleppo, where protestors demanded democratic reforms and the release of political prisoners.

By the beginning of April there had already been 22 deaths, as demonstrations spread across the country. The response of the government was violent, with tanks being deployed against demonstrators. By the end of that month there had been an additional 500 deaths, which resulted in hundreds of governing Baath Party members' resignations.[8] Things continued to spiral out of control, with over 100 people killed in a two-day period in June. By the end of the month, the cabinet had backed a draft law that allowed for rival political parties. This was the first time that such a thing had been possible in decades.

The protests continued for the rest of 2011, and in January of 2012, President al-Assad stated on television he would not resign but would stamp out "terrorists" with an iron fist. The next month, the government launched an assault on the city of Homs. By this point, violence occurring across the country had escalated well beyond simple skirmishes between the police and demonstrators and were instead what might be classified as battles of armed forces. In April of 2013, the first truce was declared in Aleppo. However, by June of that year, 4,000 Iranian troops had arrived to help the al-Assad government retain power. What had become a civil war was further complicated when al-Assad requested military aid from Russia's Vladimir Putin, who agreed to send troops. The Russian troops withdrew from Syria a little over a year later when Putin announced that the objectives of the intervention had mostly been achieved.[9]

To be clear, there were protests all over the region, including in Saudi Arabia, Yemen, Jordan, Bahrain, and Sudan. I will not detail how each of them turned out, but there were varying amounts of violence and levels of change that took place in all these countries. There is a theme that can be seen running from one country to another: A tipping point had been reached. What conditions existed in these countries that caused so much vocal, and at times violent, responses from the community? I would argue this can be traced back to the undeserving reaching a tipping point.

One of the interesting facts about the countries that comprise the Middle East and North Africa (MENA) is that before the events of the Arab Spring they were mostly considered by the West to be rather stable, although autocratically run, as highlighted in the narratives of how protests began. As Ianchovichina states, "Economic indicators tracking income growth, poverty rates, and expenditure or income inequality also presented a favorable picture and suggested that the autocratic Arab regimes had delivered on economic, human development, and shared prosperity goals."[10] As discussed in Chapter 2, there are absolute and relative measures of poverty, and MENA countries had been stable or slightly improving along several dimensions (Figure 8).

Except for the Republic of Yemen, poverty rates were falling for these economies. Using the absolute measure of poverty set at $1.25 a day, the incidence was very low for Arab Spring countries. If in the five years before the Arab Spring one examined the annual gross domestic product (GDP) of these countries, things looked promising. Tunisia, where the Arab Spring began, averaged 4.5% growth, and Morocco and Jordan averaged 5% and 6%, respectively. As Ianchovichina points out, "Economic growth in developing MENA as a whole surpassed that in Latin America and the Caribbean and in developing Europe and Central Asia."[11]

As I argued in Chapter 2, there has been a high tolerance for income inequality around the world for decades, given that there is a perceived path forward for all, namely, the social contract. Still, there have been episodes when civil unrest followed especially high periods of inequality. Some scholars view the Arab Spring as a bit of a mystery, given that economic inequality was rather low and stable in the period leading up to the mass protests of 2010 and 2011. The answer to the puzzle, from the perspective of this book, is that those individuals had reached a tipping point, and it is the composition of those who view themselves as undeserving, and not the quantity of the same, that will lead to protest. Even in the MENA region, where the social contract was different than in other parts of the world, it

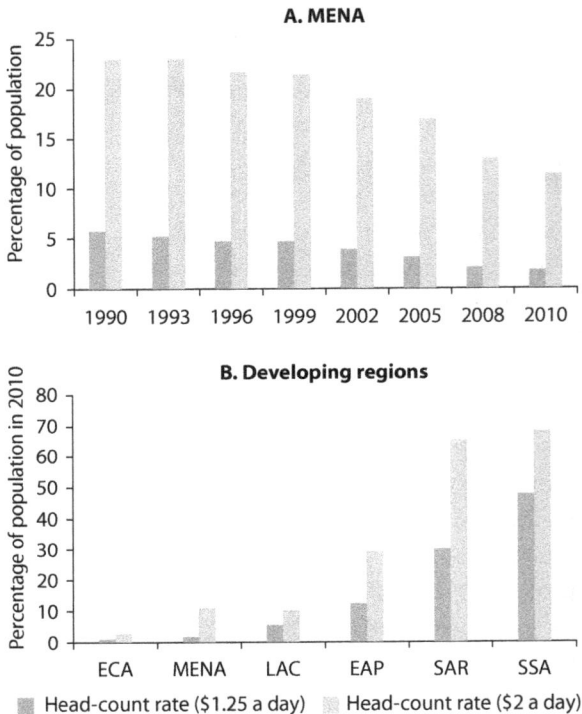

Figure 8. Poverty rates in MENA and developing regions: Europe and Central Asia (ECA), Latin American and the Caribbean (LAC), East Asia and Pacific (EAP), South Asia (SAR), and Sub-Saharan Africa (SSA). *Source:* Ianchovichina, *Eruptions of Popular Anger*, fig. O.3, citing data from World Bank PovcalNet and World Bank.

was only when the loss of resources that occurred when inequality encompassed those who felt themselves undeserving of the position had reached a critical mass did unrest occur.

Unlike the social contract I have described throughout this book, which mostly relates to the United States, the social contract that existed in the Arab Spring countries required that the government—

or, in other words, the state—provide public sector employment for those seeking it. The state was also responsible for free education and free health care.[12] As has been discussed extensively in this book, the idea of free health care is definitely not part of the social contract of the United States, although education being publicly and freely available would fit that narrative. In another departure from the US system, food and fuel costs would be heavily subsidized for all citizens. In theory, this system could lead to a great deal of economic development, given that individuals are not burdened with concerns over daily subsistence such as food, shelter, or transportation in the way that might be seen in other countries. As I will point out later, this type of system tends to squeeze out private entrepreneurial zeal, and that has drawbacks.

The social contract practiced in this region further requires that the citizenry give bureaucrats a free hand in the operation of the state. Things like corruption and graft must be overlooked as long as basic needs are being met. Even the selection of which bureaucrats hold given positions should not be questioned too extensively. In essence, the contract stipulates a trade-off of bread for silence. Citizens should not speak too loudly about autocratic, unfair, and sometimes violent acts by the state. As I mentioned in Chapter 1, the state can ensure total tranquility and order in the region, but to do so there might be few personal freedoms left, and the population must decide whether this is a worthwhile trade-off. A citizen cannot agree to abuses of personal rights and economic determination while eating the bread provided and then decide to alter the system or even speak against the system. The act of speaking out is seen as a violation of the social contract and one that might lead others to want to do the same. If a critical mass of protesters forms, then civil unrest can follow. The state is then authorized to use any force deemed necessary to stamp out engagement in such acts, or even allowing citizens to think about such acts.

The Arab Spring protester was relatively young, that is, younger than 44 years old. They were mostly, but not exclusively, men who were educated, urban and middle class. These young men were more educated than their parents and were expecting a stable source of income that would allow them to marry. Gender differences should not be thought of as a complete driver of who chose to protest, however. As Ianchovichina states,

> Progress in reducing and, in some cases, eliminating gender gaps in education, and declines in fertility rates, suggested that Arab women were more prepared than ever to participate in the labor market and contribute to economic life. The reality, however, was that unemployment rates among women were much higher than those among men, and female labor force participation rates remained low (Devarajan and Ianchovichina 2017).[13]

The region was becoming younger and promises made to this generation needed to be promises kept. There was a disconnect between generations that became vocal disenchantment. Malik and Awadallah write that "the local systems of governance remain ossified, offering limited economic mobility to the region's youth. Even physical mobility across borders is restricted. Unlike Western Europe, where class-based struggles have historically driven political change, the Middle East is witnessing a truly generational struggle for inclusion."[14]

As with all protest groups, like the Occupy Wall Street movement and the Tea Party Movement, this group of Arab Spring protestors felt that the quality of life they were promised was being compromised by corruption, and the quality of public services being provided by the government was inadequate. Like the protests in the United States, the protests in the MENA region quickly spread because of technology, which allowed the aggrieved to disseminate their message rapidly and without censor. Even though these events happened across several countries, the economic problems were fairly consistent to the populous. It is also important to note they had a common language between them.

Those people in a country most likely to protest are ones who feel put upon after adhering to the tenets of the social contract. This was definitely the case for the middle class in the period before the Arab Spring. Consider these statistics: The annual average consumption growth showed that if the income distribution was separated into three groups, comprising the lowest 40% of income earners, the middle 40% of income earners, and the top 20% of income earners, for the 40% in the middle, the income growth ranged from -3.8% in Yemen to 5.7% in Syria. Conversely, for the top 20% of income earners, the range was -4.5% in Tunisia to 31.5% in Syria. The way to interpret these statistics is that upside growth was smaller when comparing 5.7% to 31.5%. The reader should take a second to process this comparison. The 40% of people in the middle could expect to see their income grow by only 5.7%, while the smaller group of the highest 20% could expect income growth of 31.5%.[15] It is a classic example of the rich getting richer. Economists and other social scientists have often argued that a thriving middle class bolsters social and economic security for a country. When the middle is not growing much but the top is seeing incredible gains, that is not a sign of a thriving middle class. What most middle-class people in this region felt was "squeezed." It was becoming increasingly difficult to maintain middle-class status, and where would they end up if not in the middle class? They feared they would be included in an ever-increasing group of lower-income and lower–social status people. They clearly felt they did not deserve this new ordering.

As Ianchovichina notes,

> On the eve of the Arab Spring, people felt stuck. The middle class, in particular, was growing more frustrated with the quality of life in their countries. Life satisfaction scores declined markedly before the Arab Spring events, especially for the middle class in the Arab Spring countries. Arampatzi et al. (2015) associate this unhappy development with perceptions of declining standards of living, especially the deteriorating quality of public services and labor market conditions, and the growing dissatisfaction with corruption linked to the inability of people to do well without wasta, that is, connections with powerful political and business elites, particularly in the Arab Spring countries.[16]

Something had gone wrong with what the population had seen as possible for their lives. It had not been so long ago that the idea of a comfortable middle-class existence seemed possible. As Tarik Yousef, director of the Brookings Doha Center was quoted as saying in an interview with *The Washington Post*, "In 1960, the economies of Egypt and South Korea were roughly the same size. . . . Today, South Korea's economy is more than four times as large, and its population is only half the size of Egypt's."[17] It was not lost on those in the MENA region, and especially the young and middle class, that they were being left behind, and they had identified the reason as being the broken social contract.

As mentioned, the "bread for silence" type of system tends to crowd out private enterprise. The seeds of a breakdown in the social contract were planted in its very design, and the Arab Spring could probably have been predicted even if the numbers of those in poverty or the amount of inequality did not change substantially. Recall when I spoke of the composition of people on the outside as opposed to the number.

If the government or state is the employer of first and last resort, then there will clearly come a point when too many individuals are chasing too few jobs. The government can respond by continuing to bring on new employees but will have no real work for them. As long as pay is being provided, the workforce and society should not complain, because that is what the social contract states. After all, worker satisfaction was not in the social contract—only some form of pay for some form of work. It was not worker dissatisfaction that led to the revolt, but rather the lack of jobs when the state had absorbed all the people it could on the public payroll, but there were many, many more asking to be included. From that same *Washington Post* article about the Arab Spring, the writer noted, "In the 1970s, a male Egyptian graduate had a 70 percent chance of securing a government job. By 2016, that had fallen to less than 25 percent, according to calculations by Ragui Assaad, a professor at the University of Minnesota and research fellow at the Cairo-based Economic

Research Forum."[18] These were people who had adhered to the social contract and gotten the requisite degree or certificate. They also were those who had not complained, so the fact that they found themselves on the outside was disappointing and they were predictably angry.

In essence, the state had engaged in what social scientists term *elite capture*. The concept is not new. Those who are on the inside, or in the preferred group, get an outsized portion of the benefits from the social ordering. In this case, the elites captured most of the benefits from this "bread for silence" social contract and that left less to go around for those on the outside. For example, the government could be tasked with providing services like internet and computer servicing, which otherwise might have been provided by a competitive private sector. Those few elites picked by government bureaucrats, after some form of bribery had taken place, provide internet service. The elite realize they have nothing to fear from competitors and offer poor-quality products and services. They further go on to charge uncompetitive prices to the government, which are higher than they should be, and reap huge rewards in terms of high profit margins from inflated government contracts and bribes taken from other elites to ensure that services are given to them with priority. Being on the inside is good, very good.

This type of elite capture has broader impacts on the economy beyond the industry in question, with other, unrelated sectors of the economy being adversely impacted by this behavior.[19] Poor internet and computer servicing make it difficult for manufacturers to produce high-quality products, which further diminishes the size of the private sector. This behavior is especially damaging if those products being manufactured are intended for international markets. These products will be inferior in a globally competitive marketplace and will limit the size of that industry in the country. The resulting jobs available will be low-pay, low-skill, simple-assembly occupations that will frustrate the citizenry even more. This also leads to a misallocation of resources, as funds that could have been used to generate upward mobility for a large section of the population are diverted to maintaining the system of poor services and corruption. The loss of revenues from the system could not be made up by tax revenues, given the weakened private sector and graft. Grievances will only increase when a college graduate cannot find employment with the government and there are no private sector employment options matching their skill set available, so they are forced to drive a taxi or peddle merchandise on the streets.

To some extent, corruption happens in all economies and all societies. In the MENA region, with the unique nature of their social contract and fragile economic structure, the results of corruption were especially disastrous to the economy. In some countries, such as Libya, which have massive reserves of oil, the level of corruption possible was only amplified and the diversion of funds was even more exacerbated. What I term "bread for silence" is usually described by scholars who study corruption and its impact on economies as "greasing the wheels." What this means is that when institutional and governmental policies are weak, sometimes bribes and other forms of corruption are what keep the economic engine running. In other words, corruption is the grease that keeps the gears spinning. However, corruption also puts sand in the gears, which causes them to run less efficiently and eventually break down. Gründler and Potrafke explain their results:

> Corruption is negatively associated with economic growth. Real per capita GDP decreased by around 17% in the long-run. . . . The effect is especially pronounced in autocracies and countries with low government effectiveness and rule of law, supporting the "weak form" of the "grease the wheels" hypothesis. Transmission channels through which absence of corruption promotes economic growth seem to be preventing FDI and increasing instability.[20]

The "FDI" the authors were referring to is foreign direct investment. It is staggering to think of what might be possible for a country or a region with an injection of 17% more GDP. Those are the types of numbers that would capture the attention of potential investors looking for a country or region to partner with for long-term growth. The loss was sad, but predictable and avoidable.

Putting so many people on the outside and leaving them undeserving of their place was exactly what led to protest. If individuals were supposed to turn a blind eye to elite capture and corruption for the promise of government subsidies, then there was nothing but the fear of violence and coercion by the state to keep them from uniting in one voice once the subsidies were not forthcoming. The question was, what did they have to lose at this point? They could not lose a government job they did not have. They could not be put on the outside of the gravy train of bribes and corruption, since they were already on the outside. They did not need to worry about upsetting a political system that guaranteed them the right to move up the economic and social ladder, since that system did not exist.

The state recognized it could not keep up the level of subsidies and public sector employment guarantees that it had in the past, so reforms were implemented. The problem with the reforms was that the system in place was not designed to have a strong and vibrant private sector, and young people entering the job market had no place to go. They certainly were not expecting to peddle fruit on the street or work a dead-end assembly job for subsistence wages. As Malik and Awadallah wrote,

> A singular failure of the Arab world is that it has been unsuccessful in developing a vibrant private sector that survives without state crutches, is connected with global markets, and generates productive employment for its young. The region suffers from a dangerous dearth of manufacturing, best manifested in just one statistic: in 2003 the combined manufactured exports of the entire Middle East were less than those from just one South-East Asian nation, the Philippines.[21]

The comparisons between OWS, the TPM, and the Arab Spring only go so far. It is true that all were sparked by undeserving outsiders reaching a tipping point, but I would argue that the US-based protests were triggered by the financial crisis of 2008. The Arab Spring was more organic in nature and much more desperate, given the massive loss of life that occurred. Despite the violence and worldwide support for revolts happening in the region, the protestors of the Arab Spring did not win. The governments of these countries could be said to be more entrenched, violent, and corrupt now than ever before. This quote from the *Washington Post* article mentioned earlier articulates how things turned out:

> In Egypt, President Abdel Fatah al-Sissi—whose military coup in 2013 ousted the elected government that had emerged out of the Arab Spring—rules with a far tighter grip than longtime autocrat Hosni Mubarak, whose rule ended with that uprising. Today, an estimated 60,000 people are imprisoned for their political views, compared with 5,000 to 10,000 in the last years of Mubarak's tenure, according to human rights groups.[22]

If the goal of those who felt themselves as being truly undeserving was to change the system such that it would recognize their situation, then they did not achieve that goal. If the goal was to have long-lasting reforms delivered or change the nature of the social contract, then one can say with the luxury of hindsight that this goal was not achieved either. On a continuing note, there were demonstrations in 2019 in both Sudan and Algeria, which toppled long-standing presidents.[23] There were also mass protests in Iraq and Lebanon, which have been called the Second Arab Spring. One could argue that seeds were planted in the protests, and out of the failures of the Arab Spring there may yet be fruit with a new generation of citizens who want to see that promises made by the state are promises kept.

It will always be difficult to ask for this type of social contract to deliver for enough people such that the ranks of the undeserving do not swell. Elite capture, corruption, and autocratic rule will divert resources away from economic and social mobility for the masses. Unlike other forms of social contracts mentioned in earlier chapters, where the state can simply say that those at lower stations on the economic and social ladder must want to be there or otherwise they would have embraced the actions prescribed by the social contract, this system requires silencing critics, which is not seen as abusive, given that it is the contract to demand silence from inside and out. The contract never stated social and economic mobility explicitly, but it did state there would be bread for silence. When the bread stopped coming, so too was lost the promised silence.

7 Student Debt Forgiveness

Unlike the cases in earlier chapters, student debt forgiveness is a currently occurring conversation that is still evolving as of the writing of this book. The outcome of the efforts now being employed have yet to manifest themselves in society. What is clear is that higher education has a critical flaw in how it is being implemented as an action item for the social contract. We have not reached a tipping point just yet, but it would be my opinion that we are not far from one. In June of 2024, I was interviewed by CNN. The interviewer asked me about higher education and the accumulation of debt among those attending American colleges and universities. Part of what I said in that interview perfectly encapsulates the problem:

> One of the things that we tout in our society is that going to school is a way to rise up the economic and social ladder. And that by going to school and you've heard this statistic a bunch of times, that someone who goes to college, in lifetime earnings, is going to end up making at least $1 million more than someone who only has a high school diploma. And so if we're going to tell people, "look, you're going to be

better off financially if you go to college, you're going to have a better
skill set." That it is a violation when people actually come out of college more broke than when they went in. Because before, before I
went to college, I was just broke. And now, after having gone to college, I'm in debt. And I'm broke. And that's where people are becoming much, much more disillusioned.[1]

Individuals are, indeed, becoming more disillusioned with higher education in America. According to one estimate, there were more than
20 million students enrolled in postsecondary education in the United
States in 2015.[2] In 2021, that number had decreased to 15.5 million.[3]

One explanation might be that this has nothing to do with college
costs, which I will focus on later in this chapter. This could all just be
changing political views. There is some credence to that argument.
In 2010, public opinion polls told the story that college was worth
attending. In one survey, 86% of college graduates said that going to
college had been a good investment. Another survey found that 60%
said that colleges and universities were having a positive impact on
the country. Yet another poll of young adults found that 74% agreed
that college was "very important." To further the point that these
were generally universal sentiments at that time, 96% of parents
who identified as Democrat and 99% of parents who identified as
Republican said they expected their children to go to college.[4]

Going to college was seen as a good financial endeavor or, as I
have stated in this book, a vital tenet of the social contract that
assured upward mobility on the economic and social ladder. The
average American with a bachelor's degree, and no more, was making nearly two-thirds more than their high school diploma–holding
peers. This was a financial advantage that was about twice as large as
it had been a generation before.[5]

There is a wage premium that exists between individuals with a
college degree and those with only a high school diploma. The calcu-
lus of college attendance is rather simple: When employers demand
more workers with a bachelor's degree, the wage premium goes up;
however, when there is a glut or surplus of college graduates, the

premium goes down. Right after World War II, the gap between the median high school diploma holder and college graduate was about 30% with regard to wages and remained rather constant until the 1980s, when the gap began to expand. By the beginning of the 21st century, the gap had risen to 60% and now remains more or less stable around 65%. This does seem to raise a bit of a mystery, given that college enrollment has been declining, while the wage premium is rather high and steady.[6]

Things have changed. Today, only 41% of young adults think that college is very important. In addition, only one out of three Americans now says they have a lot of confidence in higher education. Furthermore, only half of American parents now say they would prefer their children attend a four-year college.[7]

It might be that the driver of the downturn in college attendance has been politics. As stated earlier, both Democrats and Republicans once held strong beliefs in the benefits of college and the value of sending their children to college. That all began to change in 2015. Tough reported that in a 2015 ongoing Pew survey, Republicans and those who lean Republican saw their view that colleges and universities had a negative impact on the country rise from 37% to 58% just in the two years between 2015 and 2017. For Democrats, the rate remained steady. In addition, a 2023 Gallop poll of Republicans found that only 19% said they had a lot of confidence in higher education, which was down from 56% in 2015. Thus, the idea that college is not "worth" it might be more of a social statement about moving up the social ladder rather than one of economic certainty that assures financial mobility.[8]

Maybe we should step back in history a few hundred years before worrying about higher education as a mode of any type of mobility and answer the following question: How did we get to this point in the first place? In other words, what is the actual history and purpose of higher education in the United States? I will endeavor to give a very brief (and thus incomplete) recounting of the ebbs and flows of colleges and universities in the country before we approach the issue of worth. There are entire wings of libraries dedicated to this topic, should the reader desire a more thorough explanation.

To begin with, less than 5% of Americans between the ages of 18 and 22 enrolled in college during the 200-year period between 1700 and 1900.[9] Our ideal of intense undergraduate education is owed to the English universities Oxford and Cambridge of the 16th and 17th centuries. These institutions earned a stellar reputation by combining several residential colleges into university structures, which were located in pastoral environments. This model came to be known as "Oxbridge" and was not like the urban models of academic life and instruction found in other urban university settings at the time in Europe. As Thelin and Gasman point out, "This model consisted of an architecturally distinct, landscaped site for an elaborate organizational culture and pedagogy designed to build character rather than produce expert scholars."[10] This point about building character should not be overlooked, because it will keep recurring in the early period of higher education in America.

There are not many records of the collegiate curriculum from the period, but experts theorize that students were put to rigorous oral disputations and were immediately taken to task by masters in the subject area and fellow students.[11]

The idea of mobility as an outcome of higher education is a rather new phenomenon. According to Thelin and Gasman, "Enrollment in college courses was confined to white males, mostly from established, prosperous families and members of each colony's dominant Protestant denomination. College attendance tended to confirm existing social standing rather than provide social mobility."[12]

Burke suggests that at the beginning of the 19th century, there were probably 25 colleges that were offering degrees.[13] The number had increased dramatically by 1860, to approximately 240 colleges, and that does not include the institutions that had started and already gone out of business. Goldin and Katz state that by 1897, the median—in other words, the number evenly splitting the population—private college student was attending an institution with 505 students and the median public college student was attending an institution with 787 students.[14] There was some separation occurring between the two groups of private and public students, but it was not as pronounced as it is now.

Part of that growth during the 19th century came about because many religious groups began the process of contemplating and building their own colleges. The reasoning was sound, given that they wanted to reinforce their doctrines among a group of individuals who were transitioning into adulthood and probably positions of leadership in the community. The colleges were designed to instill the proper set of values and the right character in these future leaders.

By the middle of the century, women had become part of the student body at colleges, although not in great numbers. The curriculum for women was different in that they had classes such as home economics and ones related to the "social graces and deportment," which might be areas of concern for women in finishing schools. However, women also received formal instruction in mathematics, science, composition, and foreign languages. These latter subjects were associated with a standard undergraduate curriculum of the time.[15]

Finally, there were already a few colleges for black individuals in the North that existed before the end of the Civil War, such as Wilberforce University in Ohio, and Cheney University and Lincoln University, both in Pennsylvania, which were established by free black people and white abolitionists. The growth in black colleges, however, was most profound between 1865 and 1910, when many small black colleges were established in the South. The funding for these new colleges came from northern philanthropic organizations, like the Peabody Foundation, but also from black churches, state governments, and the federal government through the Freedmen's Bureau. It should not be forgotten that the Land Grant Act of 1890 provided funding for 16 black colleges in the South. They were able to offer studies in agriculture and mechanical arts. Despite the Land

Grant Act and the support of private and religious groups, funding
was always uncertain and inadequate.[16]

American white males did quite fine financially without a college
education, and this persisted well into the late 19th century. A college education was seen much more as a symbol of prestige than a
badge of honor showing the diligence and determination of the
holder of a college degree. New state governments showed little
interest in funding higher education, although the granting of college charters was a convenient way for legislators to repay political
obligations.[17]

By the beginning of the 20th century, the greatest universities in
America were contributing to advancements in cutting-edge schol-
arship, and it should not be lost that this same period saw a great
deal of innovation and change in living standards, as well as industrial change for the country.[18] As Goldin and Katz state,

> In the latter part of the 19th century, an increasing number of subjects
> taught in colleges and universities became subdivided and specialized,
> and those who taught began to define themselves as occupying sepa-
> rate, specialized fields. In each subject, these changes were brought
> about by somewhat different factors and at slightly different moments
> in time. Yet several factors are common to most. They include the
> application of science to industry, the growth of the scientific and
> experimental methods, and an increased awareness of social problems
> brought about by an increasingly industrial and urban society.[19]

This is an interesting phenomenon, given that sponsored research
and graduate schools were rather limited then.[20] This period did see
universities begin to annex professional schools, such as law, medicine, business, and engineering, among others.[21] In that regard, a
university might have had a college or school of theology or phar-
macy within its overall structure, which gave students many more
options than just the classics or arts. By the turn of the 20th century,
only 48% of students who were training to be dentists, lawyers,
pharmacists, and even doctors—of both animals and humans—were

attending professional schools that were independent of other institutions of higher education. Back then, professional schools did not require that students have a college degree. Many students had not attended college at all. This all changed in the three decades following, and by 1934, only 19% of professional students were attending professional schools that were independent.[22] The federal and some state governments along with firms that had not previously hired trained chemists and physicists did so at an increasing rate. Between 1900 and 1940, the number of chemists employed in the US economy increased by more than sixfold, and the number of engineers increased by sevenfold over the same period.[23]

The name of the institution a student attended and where they received their degree always mattered, but even more delineation took place in American higher education between World Wars I and II, as some colleges and universities served the purpose of teaching a specific skill set but provided little name prestige. By this point, there were public junior colleges, normal schools, and teachers colleges, which might prepare a person for a profession but not have the cache of a "name school," such as a Yale or a Princeton. Later in the chapter, I will talk more about credentialing as a purpose of colleges, showing that students have mastered a given subject to a specific level of expertise. The degree or, in other words, the credentials received from these institutions were important and were very necessary for those attending the new slate of technical institutions that began to appear during this period. Even though there were some inroads in admittance of students from a broader swath of the population, things were nowhere near ideal:

> Individuals at the most heterogeneous institutions often encountered the most glaring conflicts, hostilities, and discrimination within the campus life. Coeducation, for example, deserves to be hailed as a positive change in promoting equity and access for women. At the same time, however, such celebration needs to be tempered with careful historical analysis of how female students were actually treated once admitted.[24]

In my field, economics, a PhD was not conferred on an African American until 1921. Her name was Sadie T. M. Alexander, and she received her doctorate from the University of Pennsylvania. The hardships she endured due to her race and gender were atrocious. After she received her degree, she found no opportunities to be a professional economist, although she considered herself as such and continued to write and give speeches about economic issues. These writings are included in *Democracy, Race, and Justice: The Speeches and Writings of Sadie T. M. Alexander*, which was authored by a close colleague of mine, Dr. Nina Banks.

Besides funding, there were other obstacles faced by the black colleges in the South, where most black Americans lived. The accrediting body, the Southern Association of Colleges and Schools (SACS), which was founded in 1895, did not have black colleges with full membership until 1957.[25] Even after 1957, there appears to be evidence that discriminatory practices continued against these schools. This was even more problematic given that a disproportionate number of black students were enrolled in and graduated from these institutions. This outcome seems especially troubling since there did not appear to be a great appetite for white colleges to admit black students, and black colleges and universities were struggling.

The percentage of college students between the ages of 18 and 22 did increase to 20% between World Wars I and II. In fact, by 1960 the figure had reached 33% and by 1970 had grown to over 50%.[26]

In the period immediately after World War II, higher education reached what many who study this area would say was its zenith, or golden age. As mentioned previously in this book, this period saw the Servicemen's Readjustment Act, or as I referred to it, the GI Bill, come into existence. There were a few unanticipated consequences of the act, given that it was much more popular than expected, but not necessarily beneficial for all veterans. There were several thousand women who were veterans, yet their receipt of the benefits promised from the act was disproportionately low. The educational benefits of the act were rather broad and could be applied across an array of educational institutions, which led to concerns about accountability and quality. There needed to be some minimum thresholds of quality for institutions receiving federal funds. Also, this tremendous influx of new students on campuses put a strain on the physical infrastructure of many campuses.

The combination of the increase of schools in urban areas, including what might be considered commuter schools, and the access to education funding due to the GI Bill led to a tremendous increase in the number of students attending higher education institutions and the influence of these institutions in society. As a consequence, more first-generation students enrolled in college than ever before. In an economy where higher-order skills and credentials were required, this new influx might have been seen as a gain for all. Even though admittance rates increased, particularly at community colleges, so did dropout rates, as those new admittees skewed toward African American and Hispanic students who were less familiar with the tools needed to navigate the higher education landscape.[27]

The decade of the 1960s saw what author Margaret O'Mara termed an "urban crisis" due to the turbulence and social upheaval of the period. In a strange way, the crisis caused university leaders and local government officials to come together in a manner unseen before that point. Generally, the term used to describe the relationship between a university and the community surrounding it is "town and gown," and that relationship has not always been a productive and mutually conducive one. As O'Mara put it, "The urban crisis had an effect on town-gown relations that endured into the early twenty-first century, not least because it made local governments and universities allies rather than adversaries."[28]

On campus, students were unhappy. The large lecture classes, due to the influx of new students, left them feeling disconnected from other students and faculty members. The physical size of campuses was increasing, and student housing became more crowded and cramped. In addition, events happening off campus were drawing their attention, like civil rights protests, the draft, and the Vietnam

War. All of this resulted in a level of student activism that had not been seen before. These years of student unrest on college campuses led to a lack of confidence from traditional supporting sources and state governments. Public officials wondered about the ability of university administrators to maintain order at their respective campuses.[29]

Off campus, university administrators were trying to manage very delicate relationships with the community. How could any university that happened to be located in an urban area not be seen as a net positive for the community? Part of the situation lay in the broad net cast for talented faculty and students by some universities, which others saw as excluding the local community and students. This has always been how my present employer, Tulane University, has been viewed by the city of New Orleans. New Orleans has always had some local students who attended the university, but many in the community view the percentage as being too small and feel, given that the university is in New Orleans, the majority of students should be from the city. School administrators view the situation differently, as they see themselves in competition with other elite private schools and must not limit themselves to the local talent pool of students. It does not help the university that it has an ugly history of racial exclusion in a city that is over two-thirds African American, which only amplifies the tensions between the community and university. In the middle of this predominantly black city is a school full of nonblack and non–New Orleans students who are highly successful and mostly from higher-income families, which leads some city officials to wonder about the value of having such an institution at all. If any research university is engaged in the chase for federal grant dollars, then national and global topics of research must be engaged in by the faculty and students, leaving local concerns by the wayside. Local communities might feel even more ignored by prominent research universities.

As O'Mara put it, "Universities are potentially 'good neighbors' or 'bad neighbors' for 'community' that may encompass a neighborhood, a city, or an entire metropolis. As economic anchors, educators, employers, and entrepreneurs, they relate to urban power structures and urban citizens on a number of dimensions and scales."[30]

The cold reality is that the modern university is much more than a bastion of learning for eager minds. It has become the economic engine that drives many cities. Maurrasse states that by the end of the 20th century, it was estimated that universities and university-affiliated hospitals and medical centers had become the largest employers in over a third of US cities.[31]

The economic enterprise that is the modern university costs a lot to operate. In addition, student expectations from a college have changed:

> Vice presidents and deans of student affairs had to face the fact that the services for which they were responsible accounted for a substantial portion of rising college costs. Whatever luxuries American higher education of the 1950s or 1960s claimed, closer inspection finds them modest and frugal in comparison to contemporary expectations with regard to such obvious services as career planning, campus security, residence hall wiring to accommodate computers, health and wellness programs, and numerous new, expanded programs and facilities for students.[32]

In our modern higher education landscape, there is an "arms race" to provide luxuries and services that will attract students. Carlson notes that this arms race has had different impacts on different types of institutions, namely, geographically isolated institutions.[33] As a result, spending on student centers, recreation centers, a variety of varsity teams, and career services has become a necessity in the goal of competing for students.

Going back to the beginning of this chapter, the answer to the riddle of declining college enrollment might lie in the question itself. Why should we examine the wages between high school and college graduates when the metric to compare might be wealth differentials? That question of wealth is precisely what has been taken up by some very good economists at the Federal Reserve Bank of St. Louis. Recall that wealth is sticky and transferable. Maybe we would draw some different conclusions if we looked at net assets, meaning the assets a person owns, such as a house or money in the bank, minus their debts, such as student loans and other payments that must be made. Researchers Ricketts, Emmons, and Kent took on this task.[34]

The task was not easy, since they had to gather data on thousands of American households. The task was further complicated by the fact that these data needed to be separated by age cohort; after all, comparing a 55-year-old college graduate to a 23-year-old high school graduate would give a very distorted picture of what was going on. They even went so far as to gather data on the racial/ethnic makeup of the person. After gathering all that data and subjecting it to rigorous analysis, a very interesting picture of college "worth" emerged.

For white individuals born before 1980, the wealth premium of having received a college degree held and was substantial. On average, their wealth was two to three times higher than that of their peers of the same race and age cohort. The story was different for white individuals born after 1980, for whom the wealth premium was not very large—meaning the accumulated wealth of college graduates was not nearly as pronounced over their white, high school graduate peers who were born in the same decade. Further, the gap was not projected to increase substantially over their lifetimes.

For black Americans, the story was similar for those with college degrees who were born before 1980, in that their wealth holdings were two to three times larger than those of their high school graduate peers. However, for black individuals with college degrees who were born after 1980, Tough writes of the Federal Reserve study,

> Black college graduates born after 1980 were experiencing almost no wealth premium at all. In fact, the researchers found that the wealth premium for Black grads disappeared even earlier than it did for the

white graduates. Black college graduates born in the 1970s weren't receiving any substantial wealth benefit, either, only those born in the 1960s and earlier. Latino families followed a similar pattern. If they were headed by someone born after 1980, they had accumulated no significant additional resources beyond those of a comparable family headed by a high school graduate.[35]

If we think of going to college as a strictly financial investment, for some the investment has not paid off as expected. In my words, the social contract has been violated. What is going wrong with this promise we have been given by society concerning higher education? Tough would argue it is the costs of attending college that impact wealth calculations, especially when substantial borrowing has to occur for the degree to be obtained:

> Carrying debt obviously diminishes your net worth through simple subtraction, but it can also prevent you from taking important wealth-generating steps as a young adult, like buying a house or starting a small business. And even if you (or your parents) were able to pay your tuition without loans, the savings you used are gone when you graduate, and thus are no longer available to serve as a down payment on a starter home or the beginning of a nest egg for retirement.[36]

The costs of attending college are much higher now, making the chance of having what people in the finance industry call a positive ROI (return on investment) less sure (Figure 9). We in economics preach there is something in the market known as the law of demand, which was alluded to in Chapter 5. Simply put, it states that as the price of a good or service rises, the demand for that good or service decreases. The reverse is also true. Going all the way back to 1931, Goldin and Katz showed that a reduction of $84 in tuition and fees at public sector institutions increased college enrollments by state residents by 1.2%.[37]

What has happened to the price of attending college today? Currently, at the University of Michigan, which is a public institution, the combined costs of tuition, fees, and other expenses for

A. Percentage of change in real tuition and fees

Percentage of change relative to 2000

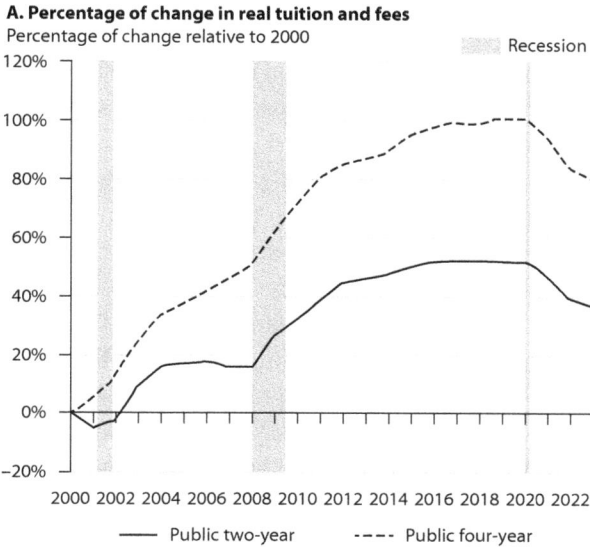

Recession

B. Percentage of change in real wage premium

Percentage of change relative to 2000

2000 wage premiums:
BA holders: 68%
Some college: 12%

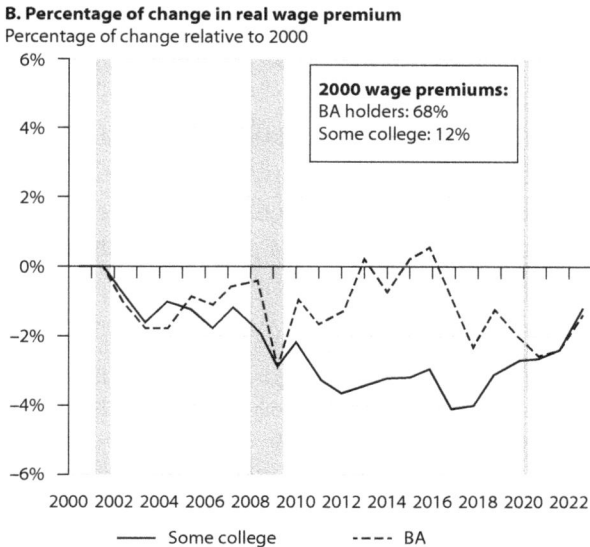

Figure 9. Changes in college costs and wage premiums relative to 2000.
Source: Council of Economic Advisors, "The Economics of Administration Action on Student Debt," fig. 1, citing data from College Board Trends in Pricing 2023, IPUMS CPS, and CEA calculations.

out-of-state juniors and seniors total in excess of $80,000 annually. There was a slight dip in costs in a few recent years, but the trend in the United States is steadily upward. In Canada and Japan, university tuition is about $5,000 annually, and even lower, at $2,000, in Italy, Israel, and Spain. According to Tough, tuition fees are virtually nonexistent in Denmark and Germany.[38]

It is not the quantity but the composition of those who find themselves on the outs that generally leads to protest. In this case, it is those who pursued higher education, as dictated by the social contract, but still find themselves coming up short. Take, for instance, that in 2007 total student debt was $500 billion, but today that number stands at a staggering $1.6 trillion. Student debt is ensnaring and burdening more and more individuals who feel they should not be included with others who did not take the proactive step to better themselves by attending college. In addition, it is becoming increasingly difficult to rid themselves of their debt—many students who took out loans between 2010 and 2019 now owe more than what they initially borrowed.[39]

Further complicating matters is the unfortunate fact that many people who start college do not finish. Now they have debts but do not have the requisite certificate to qualify for higher-paying jobs. By some estimates, as many as 40% of people who start college never finish. Tough states,

> In Federal Reserve surveys, half the borrowers who didn't finish their degrees said they were "just getting by" or "finding it difficult to get by." Two-thirds said they would have a hard time coming up with $400 to cover an unexpected expense. Financially, they were not only doing much worse than college graduates; they were doing worse than adults who had never gone to college at all. For these former students, the college wage premium had turned upside down.[40]

The social contract regarding higher education has obvious flaws, which I have tried to outline here. The most obvious question is, what are we as a society going to do about it, if anything? I will briefly discuss some efforts that have been made and are being made to help people who are not yet there but are approaching a tipping point regarding college. There are many moving parts to the student debt forgiveness plan that the government is undertaking, so some details will change and others may not reach final fruition; thus, the reader should use discretion when reading what comes next. In 2024, a federal judge froze several key parts of the plan. As discussed in the chapter regarding various aspects of the Affordable Care Act, it would be fair to assume some parts of these student debt forgiveness efforts will not survive, even if made into law. In addition, in 2025, the new Trump administration has a very different take on student debt and will presumably change all of what follows here.

One measure to correct some inherent flaws in the social contract as it relates to higher education was the Public Service Loan Forgiveness (PSLF) program, which was designed for those who work for the US federal, state, local, or Tribal government, where military service is counted as being part of the federal government. These individuals need to be employed full-time and have Direct Loans.[41] Some readers will not be familiar with the term *Direct Loan*. The website of the former U.S. Department of Education states, "Any loan received under the William D. Ford Federal Direct Loan (Direct Loan) Program qualifies for PSLF." It goes on to state that eligible loans are Direct Subsidized Loans, Direct Unsubsidized Loans, Direct PLUS Loans, and Direct Consolidation Loans. It further states,

> While a Direct PLUS loan made to a parent borrower is eligible for PSLF, it cannot be paid via a qualifying repayment plan (other than the 10-year standard repayment plan or a plan where the payment is equal or greater than the 10-year standard plan) unless it is first consolidated into a Direct Consolidation Loan. FFEL and Perkins loans may become eligible if you consolidate them into a Direct Consolidation Loan.[42]

The individual must be willing to repay the loan under an "income-driven repayment plan" and make a total of 120 consecutive qualifying monthly payments. The website went into great detail about exactly what constitutes "payment credits on consolidation loans" and what counts as a "qualifying payment"; however, I will leave the minutia to the reader who might be interested in such a plan, if they care to find it. Also, as I have mentioned before, the plans will almost assuredly change with other administrations or policy objectives, so caution is needed.

It is yet to be seen if these government efforts will provide the proper adjustments to the social contract regarding higher education, but the White House under President Biden stated that the Saving on Valuable Education (SAVE) plan, which is an example of an income-driven repayment plan, has benefit:

> The SAVE plan makes repaying college costs more affordable for current borrowers and future generations. CEA simulations show that, under SAVE, an average borrower with a bachelor's degree could save $20,000 in loan payments, while a borrower with an associate degree could see nearly 90 percent savings compared to the standard loan repayment plan.[43]

That White House gave the following example of what the SAVE plan, just the latest in a line of income-driven repayment plans, does:

> A 4-year college graduate who has $31,000 in debt and earns about $40,500 per year. Under a standard repayment plan, this borrower would pay roughly $330 dollars each month for 10 years. Under SAVE, this borrower would pay about $50 per month for the first ten years, and on average about $130 per month for the next 10 years. Over a 20-year period, this borrower would make roughly $17,500 less in payments, not accounting for inflation over that period. This represents a 56 percent reduction in total payments compared to the standard repayment plan and includes considerable loan forgiveness.[44]

They also claimed,

> Another key aspect of income-driven repayment plans like SAVE is that they protect borrowers from having to make large payments

when incomes are low. Specifically, the required payments are not based on the initial loan balance, but on one's income and household size so that those cohorts who need to borrow more to pay for college do not make larger payments unless they make more income. SAVE also protects more of a borrower's income as discretionary and, when the full plan is implemented in Summer 2024, will limit monthly payments on undergraduate loans to 5 percent of discretionary income. In fact, for single borrowers who make less than $33,000 per year, the required monthly payments will be zero dollars. From a finance perspective, the SAVE plan provides a form of insurance against tuition spikes and economic downturns—taking some of the risk out of investing in one's education while also bringing costs down.[45]

There are myriad reasons why borrowers need debt relief, but that White House added to this discussion by stating that during economic downturns, the most rapid tuition increases occur as states cut back funding to higher education and the gap is filled by tuition dollars that necessarily go up. They further stated that this is particularly problematic given that people are more likely to return to or go to college when job prospects are weaker, which is exactly what happens during an economic downturn. The Biden White House speculated that these programs, in total, would provide help to some 30 million Americans.[46]

All of this discussion about loan repayments related to higher education begs the question of what exactly a college degree implies. One explanation is that the degree could demonstrate that people have learned how to navigate byzantine and complex bureaucracies, and that might be a valuable skill in and of itself. It could be argued that college really does not teach us anything in particular but rather prepares us to learn on our own. In many settings, this skill set is handy, where the first entry-level job after college does not require a certain job skill but rather an ability to be trained for the task at hand. I have even heard that new employees are told to "forget everything you learned in school." In such a case, a college degree is nothing more than a credential that certifies that person can be trained. Many jobs come with automatic bumps in pay for each additional degree earned, even if the degree has nothing to do with the given profession. In addition, we might think of a college education as providing a value to society beyond an ability for the individual to earn a higher income. Remember that I stated the social contract should benefit the entirety of society from an individual engaging in an activity that also personally benefits them. O'Mara states, "University graduates earn more over their lifetimes, which translates into higher tax revenues, lower social service costs, and other societal benefits (Day and Newberger 2002)."[47] Further to that point, college-educated individuals are more likely to participate in a democracy, and enhanced participation might be reason enough for society to help in finding ways to defer costs so that more individuals are willing and able to attend institutions of higher learning.

We should not lose sight of what Thelin and Gasman state: "Despite the proliferation of magnificent buildings and elaborate facilities in American colleges and universities, ultimately the history of colleges and universities in this country is about teaching and learning," which is what I believe all this angst over student debt is about. Ultimately, as Thelin and Gasman write, "Although their relationship has continually evolved, students and faculty members remain the central characters in the higher education drama, without which the structures are nothing but inanimate stage props."[48]

We might want to be concerned about this issue since education, and higher education specifically, has become a tenet of the social contract. In many respects it appears education might be coming full circle—its intent during the colonial period was to make wealthy citizens, at least higher-bred white males, better leaders and more informed participants in democracy. According to Thelin and Gasman, "The American colonists built colleges because they believed in and wished to transplant and perfect the English idea of an undergraduate education as a civilizing experience that ensured a progression of responsible leaders for church and state."[49] In today's

STUDENT DEBT FORGIVENESS   133

terms, Tough writes, "For the nation's more affluent families (and their children), the rules of the higher education game are clear, and the benefits are almost always worth the cost. For everyone else, the rules seem increasingly opaque, the benefits are increasingly uncertain and the thought of just giving up without playing seems more appealing all the time."[50] This certainly sounds like this tenet of the social contract falls more in the category of a lottery than a ladder.

Without any form of correction, we might be heading for a period when only the wealthy can afford college, which the country has experienced before. The difference this time would be the economic dependence that many large cities have on thriving colleges and universities and the lightning speed with which some technology is incubated on college campuses in conjunction with technology firms. Also, we cannot ignore that in today's society a college degree has become a tenet of the social contract, whether we like it or not. This was not the case at the beginning and before the founding of the country. Since it is now, we can expect that those who feel they are undeserving of a lower rung on the economic and social ladder are going to protest their diminished status.

The tipping point that occurred, for various reasons, with Occupy Wall Street, the Tea Party, and the Arab Spring is occurring right now regarding college debt, but the seeds were planted decades ago when higher education became associated with the social contract. As the ranks of those who feel their wealth is unjustly low swell because college graduates are saddled with crippling debt, the beginning of a protest is at hand. We as a society should try to make the social contract work regarding higher education because the future is one where the need for college credentials is only going to increase. Tough reports that a 2018 report from the consulting firm Korn Ferry predicts that by the year 2030 the US labor market will have a shortage of workers with an associate or bachelor's degree, to the magnitude of 6.5 million people.[51] Others have predicted the shortfall might be as high as 8.5 million bachelor's degree holders by the end of the decade.

This emerging protest of the social contract will be interesting to observe. The costs of higher education show no signs of decreasing. The need for higher education credentials shows no signs of decreasing for those entering the workforce. If this idea of higher education is to remain as a modern precept in the context of a social contract, something is going to have to give. The numbers have just reached a tipping point, and those who feel they are on the outs or are undeserving of their station in life are beginning to coalesce around protest strategies.

8 Conclusions and Predictions

I hope the reader leaves this book understanding what I have termed the social contract. While it is not a written contract that parties could take to a court of law and use to argue for damages due to a breach, I see it is an implicit agreement between society and the individuals in it. In this context, the members of society must engage in an activity that society, as a whole, believes will benefit everyone generally, but also each person individually. Society wants to see the individual do well, since a society is a collection of individual parts. When all its parts prosper, the entire body benefits. The key here, which I have stressed throughout the book, is that there must be some action taken. This action is what distinguishes those who are worthy of the individual benefit from those who, by default, are satisfied with the status quo. The action is what will ease the burden on higher-income and higher-status members of society from being bothered with deep, probing questions about whether lower-income individuals are satisfied with their station in life. It is relatively easy to see if an individual did the action and then was rewarded with a step up the economic and social ladder. If they did not do the action, then what did they expect? Of course, they are at some lower level of the economic spectrum and are deserving of their spot.

This social contract, which many believe in religiously, goes a bit further in that it stipulates that any individual will benefit from doing the action, no matter their starting place on the economic and social ladder. In essence, the social contract assures upward mobility. This idea of assured upward mobility seems problematic on its face, and implementing it can get thorny very quickly. In this book, I tested these theoretical ideas with the data to see if they could be supported. I would argue that in the case studies in this book, the data confirms my thinking. But let's get hypothetical and build a simple society so we can see how fast issues of considerable gravity start popping up.

Let us consider two hypothetical individuals. One person has $10 and the other has $10,000. If the two individuals engage in the same activity, as prescribed by this social contract, how should society measure the benefit they were promised to receive? For instance, each could be improved by 10%, in which case the lower-income individual receives $1 for her efforts and the higher-income individual receives $1,000 for his efforts. This system might seem the fairest, given that it is proportional. After all, there was a 10% increase for everyone who engaged in the activity, regardless of their starting point. But there is more to consider, since there could also be a system of proportional-plus benefits, where there would be a 10% return for the lower-income individual and a 15% return for the higher-income individual. The lower-income individual has a total of $11 in the end, while the higher-income individual has a final tally of $11,500. This type of benefit dispersion could be justified due to the relative starting points of both. The higher-income individual could have insights that allowed him to accumulate the $10,000 in the first place. It was not random luck or nature that put him so far ahead of his less fortunate peer. He was smart, cunning, and industrious. He feels he has earned that bigger piece of the pie. Maybe the action that was required came easier to him or maybe it took him a shorter period of time to complete, thus allowing for a bit more time for his benefits to accrue. Finally, the benefit could be measured by an absolute return to the effort. In that case, both parties could get a return of, say, $100. Thus, the lower-income individual ends up with $110 and the higher-income individual has a final tally of $10,100. The beauty of all these cases is that everyone is better off because of the effort they put in. The social contract has worked regardless of the method, but can that be the only consideration? The previous chapters of this book say no.

I spent a great deal of time discussing inequality in Chapter 2, and clearly the methods described in my simple example either leave inequality as it is or increase it. It would be up to my hypothetical society to decide how they want the social contract to work, but most would agree that the implementation of the social contract is good for individuals and for society, given that in all cases everyone was better off. Even still, problems remain. What are the costs, if any, to engage in the activity? In two of the simple examples, the lower-income individual might reconsider participation if the cost to engage in the activity is more than $1, since that is all the benefit she is expecting to receive. In the last case, no one engages if the costs are greater than $100, and maybe the higher-income individual does not find engagement worth his time even for some fraction less than $100. In several chapters of this book, and especially Chapter 7, I showed that student debt might be keeping people from engaging in education as a social contract, so this is not a small concern even in my little model.

What society might want to think about doing is making access to the activity free, thus removing the cost issue entirely. The problem is that society really has not removed anything, because the costs now have been transferred and will have to be addressed through some form of taxation. I showed in Chapter 4 and especially Chapter 5 that individuals in the US context do not react positively to that type of situation. Will the tax be progressive, in that as income levels rise, individuals pay higher taxes? What about those individuals who cannot or will not physically engage in the activity? Should they be punished in some form? Another issue my society will need to grapple with is if there are situations in which benefits are mixed. In that case, the person who has engaged in the activity has a positive benefit, but it could be proportional, proportional-plus, or absolute. How would the lower-income individual feel if her efforts, which were identical to those of her lower-income peers, received a benefit of $1, while some of her peers did the same activity and had a benefit of $100? There might be calls of impropriety in the system. My society had better have an answer. In fact, society should have had this figured out before the social contract was implemented. I might be in trouble, and I only have two people to consider in my little model. Imagine how difficult and complex an issue this must be for the billions of people on the planet. This book has tried to make some sense of this.

Society is a mixture of individuals with varying abilities and skill sets. There probably should be some consideration of the task assigned in the social contract. It might simply be too difficult for some, either physically or mentally. In that case, maybe there should be multiple social contracts covering a variety of activities for participants to engage in. Can a larger set of tasks be maintained? There will have to be some ranking and consideration of which are the most important activities, which are the most beneficial to the individual and society, and which reach the widest set of people. Maybe only those activities with universal benefit are put forward as being part of the social contract, and others are merely suggested as what economists call "human capital improving," meaning they will make people better off for having engaged in the activities. In Chapter 3, I outlined several social contracts, but each had its own particular set of drawbacks.

As the reader can see, what started out as a pretty simple idea of a social contract—effort brings benefit—has grown increasingly complex before we even got going. That is what this book has been designed to explore: how using a social contract, where individuals engage in a society-endorsed activity and move up the economic and social ladder, gets complicated. The reader is probably asking more questions. What happens if the individual engages in the activity and there is no upward movement at all? The cases presented in my little model showed that benefit need not be equal, but what does society do when there is no benefit? Society might want to warn individuals of this possibility, but that means the system was not built for all, and that sounds like a lottery. The preceding chapters showed that for many people, a lottery was seen as an unacceptable conclusion, so it was excluded. Once the possibility of no reward for actions was eliminated, people became very disillusioned and sometimes protested because they were told that action always brings reward.

Will all of society just look at outcomes and make a conclusion about the deservedness of the individual? For instance, society might look at an individual who is lower on the economic and social ladder and conclude they must be happy there or else they would have engaged in the activity and moved up. Never mind that the individual did do the action but did not move anywhere. Here is the key point I hope the reader has come to understand: If society really has designed a magnificent social contract that has no flaws and works for all every time, then only those not interested in moving up, for whatever reason, would not take advantage of it. In Chapter 2 and others, I explored the idea that society is able to tolerate a high level of people who are lower on the income distribution if the belief is they are there of their own volition. Who are we to interfere with the free will of another person?

Some lower-income individuals might counter that they did, indeed, engage in the activity, but the social contract failed them— they did not fail it. They did not rise as high as their peers, or maybe they did not rise at all. How are those who did try to be distinguished from those who did not or could not try if society only looks at where they are on the economic and social ladder and not at their efforts? My model social contract could or should have had a mechanism to distinguish between the two. The middle chapters of this book deal with exactly that situation in various forms, and I should have found a way to model it here. My model society needed to have the ability to correct the error, if it truly was the fault of my social contract.

A way around fixing the social contract might be to convince the citizenry of the infallibility of the system, regardless of what was said or what people see around them. In essence, if I can convince the citizenry that these lower-income individuals failed the social contract and not the other way around, there will be no need for correction. Since this contract is not explicit, it is only as good as the faith people are willing to put into it. People need to have faith that the system works, and if I can draw a bit from religion, many acts of faith are only strengthened by having no concrete evidence to base the belief upon. In fact, the strongest proponents of a faith are those who can believe without factual evidence at all.

Without an ability to adjudicate contractual failures, since this social contract is only implicit, the system could descend into chaos. This is important because individuals might draw conclusions about my social contract from outcomes also. In other words, some people did what was expected of them but did not realize any material gain. They might be unconcerned with the fine nuances of contract law or the subtleties that make their cases unique. What they see is that society promised and did not deliver. If enough of those individuals gather together, they might reach a tipping point. If so, even my simple society might see protests, and that might explain some of the global protests we have seen over the decades. The question is whether any society up to now has learned from the lessons of the past and will be able to move forward with less conflict.

Unfortunately, I do not think we are done seeing individuals coalesce around an idea of broken social contracts and then protest loudly. I predict there will be two coming fights that will keep individuals from climbing, despite their actions.

ARTIFICIAL INTELLIGENCE

The first salvo in the coming battle over artificial intelligence (AI) and its impact on the social contract has already been fired. In the spring and summer of 2023, the Writer's Guild of America (WGA) went on strike and began negotiating with the Alliance of Motion Picture and Television Producers (AMPTP) over the terms of a contract on behalf of Hollywood studios, streamers, and production companies. The main reason was the intrusion of AI into the production of content. The WGA had proposed regulations about the use of AI as source material for the writing or rewriting of literary materials.

The dangers to the writers were clear. As Alex Hanna, Director of Research at the Distributed AI Research Institute, stated in a *Time* magazine article, "Politically, we are at the precipice of when [AI technology] will be institutionalized. Once they are institutionalized, it's hard to get rid of it."[1] The AI threat is not just an ethical one, but one about jobs. "It's not so much about what AI is going to do, but what companies are going to use AI to justify," said Myers West in the same article. Studios could have fewer people in the writers' room, with generative AI writing content that is later edited by a writer. "They could use AI to create a first draft and then bring in someone else to do a second draft. And that devalues their work by not having them do that whole process," said Meyers West.[2]

It would be a mistake to say we could not have predicted this was coming. All we needed to do was look back at our recent past to see what innovation and technology have done in the marketplace. For instance, *MIT News* put out a story about the groundbreaking research being done by David Autor, a scholar on their campus, along with a group of coauthors from around the world. The story notes that between 1940 and 2018, most of the work being done in the US was new work. However, as the article states, "'We estimate that about six out of 10 jobs people are doing at present didn't exist in 1940,' says Autor, co-author of a newly published paper detailing the results. 'A lot of the things that we do today, no one was doing at that point. Most contemporary jobs require expertise that didn't exist back then, and was not relevant at that time.'"[3]

Think about this factoid. In 1900, the famous Wright brothers, Orville and Wilbur, listed their occupation on the census form as "Merchant, bicycle"; however, in the 1910 census, they listed themselves as "Inventor, aeroplane." What changed? Their famous first flight from Kitty Hawk, North Carolina, in 1903. The job of airplane designer had not been conceived in 1900, yet by 1950 "Airplane designer" was a recognized category on the census.[4]

Some new jobs created will be the result of new technologies, and others will be the result of new consumer demands. Think of the boom in health care services for an increasingly elderly population, services that were not needed when the population was relatively younger 70 or 80 years ago. Now, having a larger cohort of trained professionals in this area is imperative. From the MIT article cited earlier, "'It's not just technology that creates new work, it's new demand,' Autor says. An aging population of baby boomers may be creating new roles for personal health care aides that are only now emerging as plausible job categories."[5]

What is impressive and troubling is that the research by Autor and colleagues shows that from the period 1940 to 1980, the jobs that were created were what might be considered "middle-class" in the areas of manufacturing and clerical employment. However, after 1980, the new jobs created have been split, in that many are high-paid professional jobs and many are low-paid service work, with a hole left where the middle-class jobs once were. The author of the MIT piece uses an interesting term, "polarization," in reference to job creation, since this seems to be the same term used most prevalently in politics also. Dizikes notes, "But in the last four decades, manufacturing started receding in the U.S., and automation started eliminating clerical work. From 1980 to the present, there have been two major tracks for new jobs: high-end and specialized professional work, and lower-paying service-sector jobs, of many types." As he points out, the US has seen an "overall polarization of occupational structure."[6] As I discussed in the last chapter, there is a fairly substantial political divide about the value of higher education in the United States. If the divide in jobs of the future falls into vastly different camps based on educational attainment, we might see the protest from education join with the protest about the need for AI in the labor market.

Autor and colleagues' research found that workers who had some college experience were approximately 25% more likely to be working in a new occupation than those who only had a high school diploma. I do not believe the coming threat of AI will only impact high school diploma holders, but it will certainly impact them harder.

Why do I think even college degree holders will be impacted by AI? Part of it has already been seen in the WGA strike, but also because the MIT article notes, "On net, the study finds, and particularly since 1980, technology has replaced more U.S. jobs than it has generated." As economist David Autor states in the article,

> AI is really different. It may substitute some high-skill expertise but may complement decision-making tasks. I think we're in an era where we have this new tool and we don't know what's good for. New technologies have strengths and weaknesses and it takes a while to figure them out. GPS was invented for military purposes, and it took decades for it to be in smartphones.[7]

Ironically, the team used some form of advanced technology in their research, so maybe even very smart MIT professors will be replaced by some form of new technology.

If things are looking different now, I predict the differences will only get more pronounced in the future. According to a study done by Price Waterhouse Cooper, by the year 2030, AI could add about $15.7 trillion to the global economy.[8] The question will be how many people will be involved in the generation of that revenue. Some will be left out and feel undeserving of that fact, given that being trained in AI was not mentioned as a necessity for upward mobility. However, things can and do change, and society better prepare its citizens for this possibility or there will be indignation over the state of affairs.

There is no doubt this is coming, but no one has sounded the alarm bells about its impact on the social contract. According to a report by the Boston Institute of Analytics (BIA), "The market for AI technologies is vast, amounting to around 200 billion U.S. dollars in 2023 and is expected to grow well beyond that to over 1.8 trillion U.S. dollars by 2030 according to Statista."[9] The BIA report also states, "The financial industry has embraced AI to automate trading, manage risk, and detect fraud. AI-powered trading algorithms can analyze vast amounts of financial data, including market trends, company performance, and economic indicators, to make informed trading decisions. This has led to increased efficiency in financial markets and improved returns for investors."[10]

The key to surviving in this new AI world will be change. The BIA report states, "While automation is causing job displacement in industries like manufacturing, transportation, and customer service, AI is also creating new job opportunities in AI-related fields like AI development, data analysis, and AI integration. These jobs require specialized skills and knowledge in AI technologies and are expected to grow in demand as AI is adopted across various industries."[11] I do not see where the social contract is telling individuals that flexibility is a necessary action required for social and economic mobility, but it should be said loudly and often.

Even though the fight has already begun in the film and TV industry, I predict that one of the next skirmish lines will happen in the transportation sector. AI is definitely going to change major components of how transportation occurs in our country, starting with the coming trend of AI-powered vehicles that are autonomous in their operation. This will mean some drastic changes in how roads are created and how traffic flows are managed. If those vehicles live up to their promise of being safer and more efficient, then society will need to make some major decisions. It will also be telling to see how society will handle the increased mobility granted to individuals who had previously been excluded from the roads due to accessibility issues.

Another coming battle, which has already been alluded to, is what AI is going to mean for the retail industry. In the *MIT News* piece, it was noted that jobs have split into high-paying technical areas and rather low-paying service jobs. Most of retail falls into the low-paying side of the ledger, and if those jobs are easily replaced by AI, where will those people go? They were identified as being less educated than their peers, so this coming AI wave will drive even more people to feel unsatisfied with their place in the economic ordering. The BIA report states,

> In the retail industry, AI is transforming the way we shop, providing personalized recommendations, enhancing customer service, and optimizing inventory management. AI-powered recommendation systems can analyze customer behavior, purchase history, and demographic data to provide personalized product recommendations. This has led to increased customer satisfaction, sales conversions, and overall shopping experience.[12]

With that type of positive feedback happening while AI is still in its infancy, this entire sector of the economy should prepare for a transformation.

HOUSING

The other major area that I predict will see a tipping point occurring in the next decade or so is affordable housing. In Chapter 4, I went over some of the circumstances that led to the housing crisis of 2008, but all indicators point to the fact that we, as a society, have not learned from the trauma caused by those events and are heading for an even greater outburst of resentment.

In October of 2021, 49% of Americans said there was a major problem with affordable housing where they lived. That was an increase of 10% from the year 2018. In that same 2021 survey, 70% of Americans agreed that younger adults have a harder time buying a home than their parents did a generation before.[13]

Between the period 2019 and 2021, household wealth grew by 30%. This number meant the median household wealth increased by $40,000 over the period. But the growth was not even. Households at the bottom 25% of the wealth spectrum saw their wealth rise by $500, while those at the top 25% of the wealth spectrum saw their wealth rise by $172,200, meaning not all households ended up seeing that 30% growth rate.[14] This point will become more important as I discuss wealth in relation to homeownership.

In January of 2022, the number of active housing listings in the US was at its lowest point in at least five years, at 408,992. That constituted about a 60% drop from the 1 million listings in February of 2020, which was just before the beginning of the global pandemic. In the fourth quarter of 2019, the national median home price (recall that the median is the number that splits the population evenly) for a single-family home was $327,100, but by the fourth quarter of 2021 that number had increased to $408,100, which constituted about a 25% increase.[15] One way to think about housing affordability is to have a ratio of one to three of the median household income and the median single-family home price. If the median house price is $400,000 in a community, then the median income should be approximately $133,000. If we find this ratio is ballooning to one to five or even one to six, then the median family will be squeezed. Everyone below will be squeezed even harder, and recall that the median refers to half the population. Looking at Figure 10, the simple takeaway is that the number of homes was decreasing and the price of homes was increasing. This was not a good combination but very predictable for economists, given the law of demand, which was discussed in the last chapter.

Our social contract has come to use the home not only as an ideal of social status and neighborhood stability, but also as a significant source of wealth. A home is generally the most expensive investment

Number of US active housing listings, by month

Median US home sale price, by month

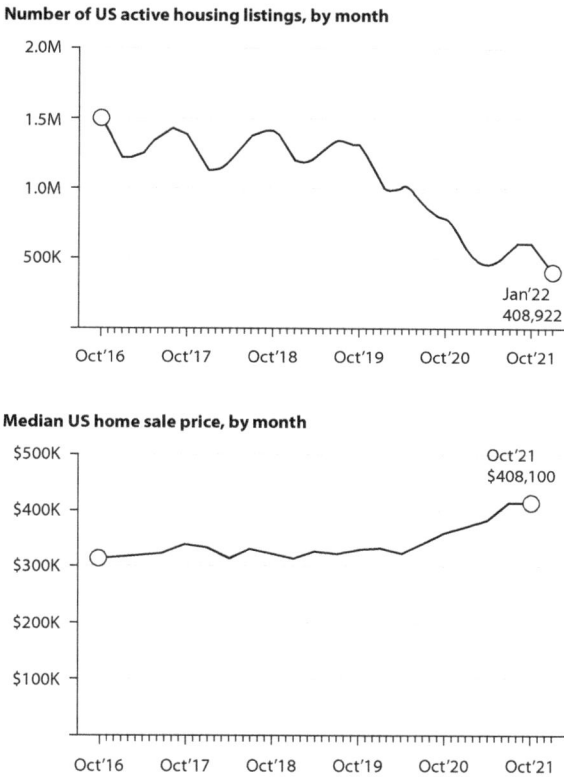

Figure 10. Home inventory and home prices. *Source:* Schaeffer, "Key Facts About Housing Affordability in the U.S.," citing data from Federal Reserve Bank of St. Louis.

most people will make in their lives and can be drawn on for help in a tough financial patch. There is a reason the home equity loan has blossomed in popularity over the past half century. Homeownership has been touted as being downright patriotic. The social contract states that owning and paying for a home is a way to move up the economic ladder, since the value of the property will help ensure access to resources needed in retirement. Thus the individual or family will not be a burden on other citizens and will show they have separated themselves from others who "only rent" and are allowing landlords to climb up the economic ladder at their expense.

The story for renting is not much better, if it is to be a stopping-off point before homeownership. If we consider renting to be the time when the individual or family saves enough money for a down payment on a starter home, then there is a problem. According to the Bureau of Labor Statistics, between 2017 and 2022, inflation added about 16% to the prices of goods and services in the US; however, during that same period, rents went up nationally by about 18%.[16] In the West rents were up 21%, and in the South they were up 20%.[17] With rent prices outpacing inflation, the burden on those trying to save for a home increased, as less money could be saved for a down payment.

This idea of a social contract around housing is relatively new, but deeply engrained these days, just like higher education. We should step back in time about a hundred years to explore the idea of publicly provided housing, which goes all the way back to the New Deal in the 1930s. Then-President Franklin Roosevelt wanted to boost the construction industry and also provide some temporary housing support for Americans. Up until World War II, the program was rather small and highly segregated, and mainly provided benefits for working-class white people. After the war ended, there was a major federal government push regarding housing to thwart a housing shortage and help with urban renewal efforts. The increased efforts saw the creation of the enormous Robert Taylor homes in Chicago, which were 28 identical 16-story buildings. This particular housing project had over 4,000 units and was the largest public housing project in the nation.[18]

Things went off course almost immediately. As Geismar notes, "Initially touted by city planners as 'palaces for the poor,' these projects experienced problems of segregation and discrimination almost from the outset and increasingly fell into disrepair due to the limited funds allocated for their initial construction and ongoing maintenance."[19] Problems really began in the 1960s, when many housing authorities changed their policies to allow single-parent households and households receiving welfare to gain occupancy. At the same time, Congress passed a law raising the cap on rents to 30% of a household's income. This substantially increased rents for working families living in the projects and caused them to exit, since rents in the private market now were comparable. The result was that with working-class and relatively higher-income households leaving, the projects became an option of last resort and were exclusively occupied by the poorest of the poor. Keller notes that "between 1950 and 1970, the average income of public housing tenants decreased from 64 to 37% of the national average (Rolnik 2019)."[20]

By the 1970s, the federal government had turned away from building large public housing projects. Instead, they embraced the private market ideas of vouchers and subsidies. This was an attempt to relieve some of the building tension regarding affordable housing. It is questionable whether these initiatives worked. Think of Section 8 housing as an example. In theory, the voucher program should have offered a host of good outcomes. It gave low-income households a voucher so they could look for housing anywhere in the city. The government would pay the rent, thus ensuring the landlord would be paid. The tenant would not be confined to a low-income neighborhood and could have neighbors who had employment and went to work daily. Seeing neighbors and having friends who had steady employment might encourage children in these households to view going to work regularly as a normal part of the day. The family would take pride in themselves and the neighborhood in which they lived. The stigma of being a low-income, publicly assisted family would be removed, since neighbors would not necessarily know the income status of the voucher recipient. In reality, Geismar notes that "while many received Section 8 vouchers to rent homes, they confronted a highly discriminatory private rental market that left many former public housing residents with few options, most of them in racially-segregated, high-poverty areas. The end result was the exacerbation of housing segregation and economic inequality in many cities, while gentrification spread."[21]

Further to that point, Keller states,

> Since 1998, the program officially goes by the name of Housing Choice Voucher Program (HCV program), because recipients are technically allowed to take their voucher and move anywhere in the country (Rosen 2020; Schwartz 2021). The only conditions are that units meet the affordability standards, pass quality inspections, and be large enough to house the number of persons on the voucher. The utilization success rate, however, is rather low. Numbers show that only 69% of voucher holders find housing within the program (Rosen 2020; Schwartz 2021). This is largely tied to landlords' skepticism.[22]

I should note it was not until the second half of the 20th century that millions of families moved out of densely occupied cities and into their own homes. This is when the home as a social contract really took root. The idea of the "American Dream" took hold during this period, when every family should have a white picket fence and 2.5 children. There were several governmental policies introduced during this period that led to the social contract being one of homeownership as a means to climb up both the social and economic ladders. Per the discussion in Chapter 4, homeownership is now viewed as a key economic driver, due to all the ancillary industries around buying and maintaining a home. In addition, ownership of the single-family variety of home is supposed to foster stronger community ties among neighbors. Keller, however, would argue that this subsidization of the suburbs led to disinvestment, segregation, and discrimination in city cores.[23]

The aforementioned policies to make homeownership a social contract include the Federal Home Loan Bank Act, which established 12 regional Home Loan Banks that oversaw the funds to help keep the mortgage market fluid and flowing. As discussed previously, when credit in the market is slowed or disrupted, great harm is incurred by all in the economy. There might be the need for bailouts, and we saw how people reacted to those. This act allowed lenders to borrow additional, secure funds from federal agencies, with the presumption being that access to these funds would make home-ownership more affordable for a larger cohort of individuals.[24]

There was also the Home Owner's Loan Corporation (HOLC), which was designed with the noble goal to help pull homeowners out of foreclosure. As Keller states about this initiative, "Essentially, the aim was to purchase default loans using federal funds. The home-owners then received a new payment plan to reduce the monthly costs, which stretched over a period of initially 15 years and later up to 30 years—compared to 11 years before the Depression. Thereby, the HOLC changed the housing finance system forever. The 30-year mortgage payment plan is still predominant today."[25]

Another government agency designed to help stimulate housing construction was the Federal Housing Administration (FHA). The FHA was designed to insure mortgages offered by qualified lenders. As I wrote in Chapter 4, the mortgage lender needed not be overly concerned about borrowers who failed to repay their loan balance because the FHA would step in to cover the difference. The rationale behind this initiative was that the mortgage lender would not lose their capital in the event of a default by the borrower, which meant that more loans could be offered, at presumably lower interest rates. More and more individuals would have access to mortgages, and the social contract would become a reality for most. I use the word *most* and not *all* because of redlining. As mentioned in Chapter 1, it is a practice that is illegal now but happened with great frequency. Keller provides a great explanation of what it was and how it impacted the social contract:

> In particular, the HOLC and the FHA had a clear bias toward lending money to white households who sought to purchase a home in a sub-urban neighborhood. . . . They developed the so-called Residential Security Maps, which showed where it was "safe" to secure a mort-gage. The maps rated all residential neighborhoods in a city or juris-diction according to their safety, establishing four categories: the first and most desirable grade A being marked in green, grade B in blue, grade C in yellow, and finally grade D in red. For this reason, the

practice came to be known as redlining, as those neighborhoods that were deemed "hazardous" were marked in red on the map.[26]

One other organization worth mentioning is the Federal Housing National Mortgage Association, better known as Fannie Mae. This institution was also mentioned in previous chapters. Its purpose was to purchase FHA-insured mortgages to refinance them, thus increasing the liquidity, or cash flow, of the FHA. As Keller notes, "Hence, the system of secondary mortgage lending was introduced, as the mortgage no longer stayed with one institution (Heeg and Reithmeier 2017). This has particularly shaped the housing market in the late twentieth century."[27] I would argue that the Great Recession has shown the consequence, unintended or unforeseen, of these actions.

Finally, there should be mention again of the Veterans Administration (VA)–backed loans, which emerged from the GI Bill. The implications of this act went far beyond college education.

The reason I see this issue of housing rising to the level of what we saw with Occupy Wall Street, the Tea Party, and the Arab Spring is that people have to live somewhere. We simply cannot expect to function as a society with large portions of our population unhoused. We have clearly and forever more turned away from affordable public housing, and the private housing market is becoming increasingly out of reach except for those at the very top of the income spectrum. This means that half the population or more has no place to affordably lay their heads, and yet society keeps pushing the idea that homeownership is a necessary action of the social contract.

I should point out something that is touted in the fields of economics, science, and engineering, along with many others, about system design. If an individual designs a system, or in my words, a social contract, the same input must repeatedly and predictably produce the same output. If the same input cannot be counted on to give the same output, then there is a design flaw and some thought should be given to a redesign. At a minimum, the user should be made aware of the glitch in the system. What I hope the reader has taken away from this book is that many in our society are not willing to admit there is a glitch in the system at all. They simply attribute the problem to the end users. My training in economics and mathematics has a problem with that logic. Simply put, if there are 45 million individuals at substantially lower rungs of the economic ladder, it is statistically inconceivable that so many are suffering from a culture or pathology that keeps them from climbing. Even if we can find success stories for hundreds or thousands or hundreds of thousands, the numbers still do not add up when there are millions left behind. It is hard to imagine that of the millions of people still at the lower rungs of the economic ladder, not one of them tried to climb and they are all satisfied with their current position. It is more conceivable that some tried to climb but were not successful. If that is the case, then the system is not working as intended, and instead of a ladder what we actually have is a lottery.

In the end, I do not see the steadfast belief in the social contract ending anytime soon. Because individuals have the ingrained belief that the system is there and works perfectly, some will inevitably be disappointed and disillusioned when fault lines appear in the solid foundation of the social contract. When enough people come to the same conclusion and a tipping point is reached, there will be an outcry. Will they be heard? Will there be change? That, even I am not able to predict. Maybe I will need to rewrite this book and draw a different conclusion if that ever occurs.

Notes

1. WHO ARE THE HAVES AND HAVE NOTS?

1. Gary A. Hoover and Erik O. Kimbrough, "An Experimental Study of the Impact of Social Comparison on Investment," *Social Science Quarterly* 97, no. 2 (2016): 350–61, https://doi.org/10.1111/ssqu.12228.

2. Hoover and Kimbrough, "Experimental Study," 360.

3. Michael B. Katz, *The Undeserving Poor: America's Enduring Confrontation with Poverty*, 2nd ed. (Oxford: Oxford University Press, 2013).

4. Katz, *Undeserving Poor*, 3.

5. Gary A. Hoover, "When User Error Calls for a Product Redesign: Poverty in the United States," *Southern Economic Journal* 91, no. 4 (2025): 1208–12, https://doi.org/10.1002/soej.12726.

6. Neil Bhutta et al., "Disparities in Wealth by Race and Ethnicity in the 2019 Survey of Consumer Finances," *FEDS Notes*, Board of Governors of the Federal Reserve System, September 28, 2020, https://doi.org/10.17016/2380-7172.2797.

7. Ellora Derenoncourt et al., "Wealth of Two Nations: The U.S. Racial Wealth Gap, 1860–2020," *Quarterly Journal of Economics* 139, no. 2 (May 2024): 693–750, https://doi.org/10.1093/qje/qjad044.

8. William Darity Jr. et al., *What We Get Wrong About Closing the Racial Wealth Gap* (Durham, NC: Samuel DuBois Cook Center on Social Equity, April 2018), 6.

9. Aditya Aladangady et al., "Greater Wealth, Greater Uncertainty: Changes in Racial Inequality in the Survey of Consumer Finances," *FEDS Notes*, Board of Governors of the Federal Reserve System, October 18, 2023, https://doi.org/10.17016/2380–7172.3405.

2. POVERTY AND INEQUALITY BY THE NUMBERS

1. *Poverty: The History of a Measure* (Washington, DC: United States Census Bureau, January 2014).

2. *How the Census Bureau Measures Poverty* (Washington, DC: United States Census Bureau, 2021).

3. *History of a Measure*.

4. *How the Census Bureau Measures Poverty*.

5. Joe Hasell, "From $1.90 to $2.15 a Day: The Updated International Poverty Line," Our World in Data, last modified October 17, 2022, https://ourworldindata.org/from-1-90-to-2-15-a-day-the-updated-international-poverty-line.

6. Hasell, "International Poverty Line."

7. Hasell, "International Poverty Line."

8. Hasell, "International Poverty Line."

9. Simon Kuznets, "Economic Growth and Income Inequality," *American Economic Review* 34, no. 1 (1955): 1–28.

10. "Farm Population Lowest Since 1850's," *New York Times*, July 20, 1988, https://www.nytimes.com/1998/07/20/us/farm-population-lowest-since-1850-s.html.

11. David S. Landes, *The Unbound Prometheus* (Cambridge: Cambridge University Press, 1969), 60.

12. Jon D. Wisman, "How the Bourgeoisie's Quest for Status Placed Blame for Poverty on the Poor," Working paper (American University Department of Economics, March 2022).

13. Ron Haskins, "Decisions That Doom the Future," *Washington Post*, March 30, 2012.

14. Alberto Alesina et al., "Why Doesn't the United States Have a European-Style Welfare State?," *Brookings Papers on Economic Activity* 32, no. 2 (2001): 187–278.

15. Alberto Alesina and Eliana La Farrara, "Preferences for Redistribution in the Land of Opportunities," Working paper 8267 (National Bureau of Economic Research, May 2001).

3. SOCIAL CONTRACTS IN THEORY AND PRACTICE

1. Claudia Goldin, "A Brief History of Education in the United States," Working paper (National Bureau of Economic Research, August 1999), 1, http://doi.org/10.3386/h0119.

2. Goldin, "Brief History of Education," 1.

3. Jacqueline Palachko et al., "How ZIP Codes Determine the Quality of a Child's Education," AP, November 9, 2019, https://apnews.com/article/1d 856cd98d4c491e8443576b3a817740.

4. Brianna McGurran, "College Tuition Inflation: Compare the Cost of College Over Time," *Forbes*, May 9, 2023, https://www.forbes.com/advisor /student-loans/college-tuition-inflation/.

5. Sandro Galea and Nason Maani, "The Cost of Preventable Disease in the USA," *Lancet Public Health* 5, no. 10 (October 2020): e513–14, https:// doi.org/10.1016/S2468-2667(20)30204-8.

6. David E. Bloom et al., "Health and Economic Growth: Reconciling the Micro and Macro Evidence," Working paper 26003 (National Bureau of Economic Research, June 2019, revised June 2022).

7. "The Causes and Costs of Absenteeism in the Workplace," *Forbes*, last updated April 14, 2022, https://www.forbes.com/sites/investopedia /2013/07/10/the-causes-and-costs-of-absenteeism-in-the-workplace.

8. Michael Sainato, "'I Live on the Street Now': How Americans Fall into Medical Bankruptcy," *The Guardian*, November 14, 2019, https:// www.theguardian.com/us-news/2019/nov/14/health-insurance-medical-bankruptcy-debt.

9. Sainato, "'I Live on the Street Now.'"

10. Alaya Hinton, "Don't Become a Parent Until You've Hit These Money Milestones," The Balance, October 20, 2021, https://www.thebalance-money.com/money-milestones-before-having-kids-4144742.

11. Douglas Martin, "James R. Dumpson, a Defender of the Poor, Dies at 103," *New York Times*, November 8, 2012, https://www.nytimes .com/2012/11/09/nyregion/james-r-dumpson-a-defender-of-the-poor-dies-at-103.html.

12. "Truth #5: There Are Many Reasons Women Have Children; Increased Benefits Isn't One of Them," Voices of Welfare, accessed November 11, 2023, https://blogs.elon.edu/voicesofwelfare/truth-5-there-are-many-reasons-women-have-children-increased-benefits-isnt-one-of-them/.

13. Anna Brown, *More Childless U.S. Adults Now Say They Don't Plan to Ever Have Kids* (Washington, DC: Pew Research Center, November 19, 2021).

14. *2020 Small Business Profile*, Office of Advocacy, U.S. Small Business Administration, June 2020, https://advocacy.sba.gov/wp-content/uploads/2020/06/2020-Small-Business-Economic-Profile-US.pdf.

15. *2020 Small Business Profile.*

16. Vivian Tuong, "6 Incredible Businesses That Started in a Garage," American Express, last updated August 14, 2023, https://www.americanexpress.com/en-us/business/trends-and-insights/articles/6-incredible-companies-that-started-in-a-garage/.

17. Surekha Carpenter, "Expanding Credit Access through Community Development Financial Institutions," Federal Reserve Bank of Richmond, Econ Focus, Fourth Quarter 2022, 27.

18. Carpenter, "Expanding Credit Access," 28.

19. Carpenter, "Expanding Credit Access," 28.

20. Sabrina T. Howell et al., "Lender Automation and Racial Disparities in Credit Access," Working paper 29364 (National Bureau of Economic Research, October 2021, revised November 2022), 25.

21. Elizabeth Brown and Austin Nicholls, *Self-Employment, Family-Business Ownership, and Economic Mobility*, Urban Institute, May 2014.

22. "Establishment Age and Survival Data," U.S. Bureau of Labor Statistics, accessed November 3, 2023, https://www.bls.gov/bdm/bdmage.htm.

23. "G. I. Bill," History.com, last updated May 27, 2010, https://www.history.com/topics/world-war-ii/gi-bill.

24. "G. I. Bill."

25. "Naturalization Through Military Service," U.S. Citizenship and Immigration Services, accessed December 1, 2023, https://www.uscis.gov/military/naturalization-through-military-service.

26. "About GI Bill Benefits," U.S. Department of Veterans Affairs, accessed December 1, 2023, https://www.va.gov/education/about-gi-bill-benefits/.

4. OCCUPY WALL STREET

1. "About TARP," U.S. Department of the Treasury, accessed January 5, 2024, https://home.treasury.gov/data/troubled-assets-relief-program/about-tarp.

2. "About TARP."

3. "About TARP."

4. "About TARP."

5. Steve Liesman, "TARP Executive Compensation Limits Set at $500,000," CNBC, last modified August 5, 2010, https://www.cnbc.com/id/29003965/.

6. Christy L. Romero, "The Special Master's Determinations for Executive Compensation of Companies Receiving Exceptional Assistance Under TARP, Special Inspector General for Troubled Asset Relief Program," Official memorandum (Office of the Special Inspector General for the Troubled Asset Relief Program, January 23, 2012), https://fraser.stlouisfed.org/title/special-master-s-determinations-executive-compensation-companies-receiving-exceptional-assistance-tarp-5101.

7. Romero, "Special Master's Determinations."

8. Sharada Dharmasankar and Bhashkar Mazumder, "Have Borrowers Recovered from Foreclosures During the Great Recession?," *Chicago Fed Letter*, no. 370, Federal Reserve Bank of Chicago, 2016.

9. "Occupy Wall Street: A Protest Timeline," *The Week*, last updated November 21, 2011, https://web.archive.org/web/20140209113047/http:/theweek.com/article/index/220100/occupy-wall-street-a-protest-timeline.

10. "Occupy Wall Street: A Protest Timeline"; "Facts About Occupy Wall Street," Occupy Wall Street, October 28, 2019, http://occupywallst.org/.

11. Arindrajit Dube and Ethan Kaplan, "Occupy Wall Street and the Political Economy of Inequality," *Economist's Voice* 3, no. 9 (March 2012): 1.

12. Hannah Shaw and Chad Stone, *Tax Data Show Richest 1 Percent Took a Hit in 2008, but Income Remained Highly Concentrated at the Top*, Center on Budget and Policy Priorities, last updated May 25, 2011, https://www.cbpp.org/research/tax-data-show-richest-1-percent-took-a-hit-in-2008-but-income-remained-highly-concentrated.

13. Dube and Kaplan, "Occupy Wall Street," 1.

14. Dube and Kaplan, "Occupy Wall Street," 2.

15. Dube and Kaplan, "Occupy Wall Street," 2.

16. Dube and Kaplan, "Occupy Wall Street," 2.

17. "Occupy Wall Street: A Protest Timeline."

18. *Wealth Gaps Rise to Record Highs Between Whites, Blacks, Hispanics* (Washington, DC: Pew Research Center, July 26, 2011), https://www.pewresearch.org/social-trends/2011/07/26/wealth-gaps-rise-to-record-highs-between-whites-blacks-hispanics/.

19. Kenyan Farrow, "Occupy Wall Street's Race Problem," The American Prospect, October 24, 2011, https://prospect.org/civil-rights/occupy-wall-street-s-race-problem/.

20. James A. Anderson, "Some Say Occupy Wall Street Did Nothing: It Changed Us More than We Think," *Time*, November 15, 2021, https://time.com/6117696/occupy-wall-street-10-years-later/.

21. "Occupy Wall Street: A Protest Timeline."

5. THE TEA PARTY

1. Walter E. Williams, "Quotes," AZ Quotes, accessed January 29, 2024, https://www.azquotes.com/author/18339-Walter_E_Williams.

2. "About the ACA," U.S. Department of Health and Human Services, last modified March 17, 2022, https://www.hhs.gov/healthcare/about-the-aca/index.html.

3. "About the ACA."

4. Lena Borrelli, "What Is the Affordable Care Act (Obamacare)?," *Forbes*, last modified February 15, 2024, https://www.forbes.com/advisor/health-insurance/what-is-obamacare/.

5. *The Budget and Economic Outlook: Fiscal Years 2013 to 2023*, Congressional Budget Office, February 2013, https://www.cbo.gov/sites/default/files/113th-congress-2013–2014/reports/43907-BudgetOutlook.pdf.

6. "Full List of Obamacare Tax Hikes," accessed January 29, 2024, https://jeffduncan.house.gov/full-list-obamacare-tax-hikes.

7. Matthew Fiedler, "The ACA's Individual Mandate in Retrospect: What Did It Do, and Where Do We Go from Here?," *Health Affairs* 39, no. 3 (2020): 429–35.

8. An Act to Provide for Reconciliation Pursuant to Titles II and V of the Concurrent Resolution on the Budget for Fiscal Year 2018, H.R.1, 115th Cong. (2017–2018).

9. Brian O'Connell, "Taxes and the Affordable Care Act," Investopedia, last modified September 6, 2023, https://www.investopedia.com/articles/personal-finance/020714/new-taxes-under-affordable-care-act.asp.

10. Marcus Hawkins, "The History of the Tea Party from Its Beginning to Now," Thoughtco, last modified October 27, 2019, https://www .thoughtco.com/a-history-of-the-tea-party-movement-3303278.

11. Jessica Eastland-Underwood, "What Was the Original Intent? The Tea Party Movement, the Founding Fathers, and the American Welfare State," *Journal of Political Ideologies* 28, no. 2 (2023): 221, https://doi.org /10.1080/13569317.2021.1956758.

12. Kimberly Amadeo, "The Tea Party Movement, Its Economic Platform and History," The Balance, last modified March 4, 2021, https://www.thebalancemoney.com/tea-party-movement-economic-platform-3305571.

13. Michael Ray, "Tea Party Movement," *Britannica*, last modified July 27, 2024, https://www.britannica.com/topic/Tea-Party-movement.

14. Eastland-Underwood, "Original Intent," 223.

15. Hawkins, "History of the Tea Party."

16. Tom Cohen, "5 Years Later, Here's How the Tea Party Changed Politics," CNN Politics, last modified February 28, 2014, https://www.cnn .com/2014/02/27/politics/tea-party-greatest-hits/index.html.

17. Eastland-Underwood, "Original Intent," 225.

18. Gary A. Hoover, "Elected Versus Appointed School District Officials: Is There a Difference in Student Outcomes?," *Public Finance Review* 36, no. 5 (2008): 635–47.

19. Todd Gitlin, "The Left Declares Its Independence," *New York Times*, October 8, 2011, https://www.nytimes.com/2011/10/09/opinion/sunday /occupy-wall-street-and-the-tea-party.html.

20. Amadeo, "Tea Party Movement."

21. James A. Anderson, "Some Say Occupy Wall Street Did Nothing: It Changed Us More than We Think," *Time*, November 15, 2021, https://time .com/6117696/occupy-wall-street-10-years-later/.

22. Anderson, "Occupy Wall Street ."

23. Eastland-Underwood, "Original Intent," 223.

24. Eastland-Underwood, "Original Intent," 219.

6. THE ARAB SPRING

1. Ali Akbar, "The Green Movement in Iran: Reformist Roots and Objective," *Protest* 1 (2021): 31.

2. Akbar, "Green Movement," 33.

3. Akbar, "Green Movement," 34–35.

4. *Britannica*, "Arab Spring," last modified July 13, 2024, https://www
.britannica.com/event/Arab-Spring.

5. "Timeline: How the Arab Spring Unfolded," Al Jazeera, last modified
January 14, 2021, https://www.aljazeera.com/news/2021/1/14/arab-spring-
ten-years-on.

6. "How the Arab Spring Unfolded."

7. "How the Arab Spring Unfolded."

8. "How the Arab Spring Unfolded."

9. "How the Arab Spring Unfolded."

10. Elena Ianchovichina, *Eruptions of Popular Anger: The Economics of
the Arab Spring and Its Aftermath*, MENA Development Report (Washington, DC: World Bank, 2018), https://doi.org/10.1596/978-1-4648-1152-4.

11. Ianchovichina, *Eruptions*, 1.

12. Adnan Mazarei and Tokhir Mirzoev, "Four Years After the Spring,"
Finance & Development 52, no. 2 (June 2015).

13. Ianchovichina, *Eruptions*, 14.

14. Adeel Malik and Bassem Awadallah, "The Economics of the Arab
Spring," *World Development* 45 (2013): 297.

15. Ianchovichina, *Eruptions*, 11.

16. Ianchovichina, *Eruptions*, 11.

17. Liz Sly, "The Unfinished Business of the Arab Spring," *Washington
Post*, January 24, 2021, https://www.washingtonpost.com/world/interactive
/2021/arab-spring-10-year-anniversary-lost-decade/.

18. Sly, "Unfinished Business."

19. Mazarei and Mirzoev, "Four Years After the Spring."

20. Klaus Gründler and Niklas Potrafke, "Corruption and Economic
Growth: New Empirical Evidence," *European Journal of Political Economy* 60 (2019): 10.

21. Malik and Awadallah, "Economics of the Arab Spring," 296.

22. Sly, "Unfinished Business."

23. *Britannica*, "Arab Spring."

7. STUDENT DEBT FORGIVENESS

1. Audie Cornish, host, *The Assignment with Audie Cornish*, podcast,
"The Economy's Bad Vibes," CNN, May 30, 2024, https://www.cnn
.com/audio/podcasts/the-assignment/episodes/909eece6-ae4a-11ee-8467-
d3288baf1c6f.

2. John Thelin and Marybeth Gasman, "The History of Student Affairs at Colleges and Universities," in *Student Affairs: A Handbook for the Professions*, ed. John Schuh, Susan Jones, and Shaun R. Harper (San Francisco: Jossey-Bass, 2011).

3. Paul Tough, "Americans Are Losing Faith in the Value of College: Whose Fault Is That?," *New York Times Magazine*, September 5, 2023, https://www.nytimes.com/2023/09/05/magazine/college-worth-price.html.

4. Tough, "Losing Faith."

5. Tough, "Losing Faith."

6. Tough, "Losing Faith."

7. Tough, "Losing Faith."

8. Tough, "Losing Faith."

9. Thelin and Gasman, "Student Affairs."

10. Thelin and Gasman, "Student Affairs," 5.

11. Thelin and Gasman, "Student Affairs," 6.

12. Thelin and Gasman, "Student Affairs," 6.

13. Colin B. Burke, *American Collegiate Populations: A Test of the Traditional View* (New York: New York University Press, 1982).

14. Claudia Goldin and Lawrence F. Katz, "The Shaping of Higher Education: The Formative Years in the United States, 1890 to 1940," *Journal of Economic Perspectives* 13, no. 1 (1999): 43.

15. Thelin and Gasman, "Student Affairs," 7.

16. Thelin and Gasman, "Student Affairs," 8.

17. Thelin and Gasman, "Student Affairs," 7.

18. Thelin and Gasman, "Student Affairs," 9.

19. Goldin and Katz, "Shaping of Higher Education," 38.

20. Goldin and Katz, "Shaping of Higher Education," 45.

21. Thelin and Gasman, "Student Affairs," 9.

22. Goldin and Katz, "Shaping of Higher Education," 46.

23. David L. Kaplan and M. Claire Casey, *Occupational Trends in the United States, 1900 to 1950*, Bureau of the Census Working Paper No. 5 (Washington, DC: Government Printing Office, 1958).

24. Thelin and Gasman, "Student Affairs," 10.

25. Thelin and Gasman, "Student Affairs," 8.

26. Thelin and Gasman, "Student Affairs," 4.

27. Thelin and Gasman, "Student Affairs," 12.

28. Margaret P. O'Mara, "Beyond Town and Gown: University Economic Engagement and the Legacy of the Urban Crisis," *Journal of Technology Transfer* 37, no. 2 (April 2012): 234.

29. Thelin and Gasman, "Student Affairs," 13.

30. O'Mara, "Town and Gown," 235.

31. David Maurrasse, *Beyond the Campus: How Colleges and Universities Form Partnerships with Their Communities* (New York: Routledge, 2001).

32. Thelin and Gasman, "Student Affairs," 15.

33. Scott Carlson, "Spending Shifts as Colleges Compete on Students' Comfort," *Chronicle of Higher Education* (August 1, 2014): 20–23.

34. Tough, "Losing Faith."

35. Tough, "Losing Faith."

36. Tough, "Losing Faith."

37. Goldin and Katz, "Shaping of Higher Education," 56.

38. Tough, "Losing Faith."

39. Tough, "Losing Faith."

40. Tough, "Losing Faith."

41. "Public Service Loan Forgiveness," Federal Student Aid, accessed June 12, 2024, https://studentaid.gov/manage-loans/forgiveness-cancellation /public-service.

42. "Public Service Loan Forgiveness."

43. Council of Economic Advisors, "The Economics of Administration Action on Student Debt," April 8, 2024, https://www.whitehouse.gov/cea /written-materials/2024/04/08/the-economics-of-administration- action-on-student-debt/; "6 Things You Should Know about the SAVE Plan," Federal Student Aid, accessed June 12, 2024, https://studentaid .gov/articles/6-things-to-know-about-save/.

44. Council of Economic Advisors, "Economics of Administration Action."

45. Council of Economic Advisors, "Economics of Administration Action."

46. Council of Economic Advisors, "Economics of Administration Action."

47. O'Mara, "Town and Gown," 238.

48. Thelin and Gasman, "Student Affairs, 3.

49. Thelin and Gasman, "Student Affairs, 5.

50. Tough, "Losing Faith."

51. Tough, "Losing Faith."

8. CONCLUSIONS AND PREDICTIONS

1. Simone Shah, "The Writers' Strike Is Taking a Stand on AI," *Time*, last modified May 4, 2023, https://time.com/6277158/writers-strike- ai-wga-screenwriting/.

2. Shah, "Writers' Strike."

3. Peter Dizikes, "Most Work Is New Work, Long-Term Study of U.S. Census Data Shows," *MIT News*, April 1, 2024, https://news.mit.edu/2024 /most-work-is-new-work-us-census-data-shows-0401.

4. Dizikes, "Most Work."

5. Dizikes, "Most Work."

6. Dizikes, "Most Work."

7. Peter Dizikes, "Does Technology Help or Hurt Employment?," *MIT News*, April 1, 2024, https://news.mit.edu/2024/does-technology-help-or-hurt-employment-0401.

8. *Sizing the Prize: What's the Real Value of AI for Your Business and How Can You Capitalise?* (London: Price Waterhouse Cooper, 2017), https://www.pwc.com/gx/en/issues/analytics/assets/pwc-ai-analysis-sizing-the-prize-report.pdf.

9. "The Future of AI: How Artificial Intelligence Will Change the World," Boston Institute of Analytics, March 28, 2024, https://bostoninstituteof analytics.org/blog/the-future-of-ai-how-artificial-intelligence-will-change-the-world/.

10. "The Future of AI."

11. "The Future of AI."

12. "The Future of AI."

13. Katherine Schaeffer, "Key Facts About Housing Affordability in the U.S," Pew Research Center, March 23, 2022, https://www.pewresearch .org/short-reads/2022/03/23/key-facts-about-housing-affordability-in-the-u-s/.

14. Kamaron McNair, "Household Wealth Grew 30% Between 2019 and 2021—Here's Who Gained the Most," MSN, December 9, 2023, https://www.msn.com/en-us/money/markets/household-wealth-grew-30-between-2019-and-2021-heres-who-gained-the-most/ar-AA1lfiV6.

15. Schaeffer, "Housing Affordability."

16. "Consumer Price Index for All Urban Consumers: Rent of Primary Residence in West," FRED, Federal Reserve Bank of St. Louis, accessed August 1, 2024, https://fred.stlouisfed.org/graph/?g = G6ea.

17. Schaeffer, "Housing Affordability."

18. Lily Geismar, "America Needs a New Approach on Affordable Housing: History Offers a Guide," *Time*, March 25, 2024, https://time .com/6900050/public-housing-biden-plan-history/.

19. Geismar, "America Needs a New Approach."

20. Judith Keller, "A Brief History of Housing in the USA," in *The US Housing Crisis: Home and Trust in the Real Estate Economy* (Cham:

SpringerNatureSwitzerland,2024),https://doi.org/10.1007/978-3-031-57758-1_4.

  21. Geismar, "America Needs a New Approach."

  22. Keller, "Brief History," 75.

  23. Keller, "Brief History," 66.

  24. Keller, "Brief History," 68.

  25. Keller, "Brief History," 68.

  26. Keller, "Brief History," 72–73.

  27. Keller, "Brief History," 68.

Bibliography

Akbar, Ali. "The Green Movement in Iran: Reformist Roots and Objective." *Protest* 1 (2021): 29–53.

Al Jazeera. "Timeline: How the Arab Spring Unfolded." Last modified January 14, 2021, https://www.aljazeera.com/news/2021/1/14/arab-spring-ten-years-on.

Aladangady, Aditya, Andrew C. Chang, and Jacob Krimmel. "Greater Wealth, Greater Uncertainty: Changes in Racial Inequality in the Survey of Consumer Finances." *FEDS Notes*, Board of Governors of the Federal Reserve System, October 18, 2023. https://doi.org/10.17016/2380–7172 .3405.

Alesina, Alberto, Edward Glaeser, and Bruce Sacerdote. "Why Doesn't the United States Have a European-Style Welfare State?" *Brookings Papers on Economic Activity* 32, no. 2 (2001): 187–278.

Alesina, Alberto, and Eliana La Ferrara. "Preferences for Redistribution in the Land of Opportunities." Working paper 8267, National Bureau of Economic Research, May 2001.

Amadeo, Kimberly. "The Tea Party Movement, Its Economic Platform and History." The Balance, last modified March 4, 2021. https://www .thebalancemoney.com/tea-party-movement-economic-platform-3305571.

Anderson, James A. "Some Say Occupy Wall Street Did Nothing: It Changed Us More than We Think." *Time*, November 15, 2021. https://time.com/6117696/occupy-wall-street-10-years-later/.

AZ Quotes. Walter E. Williams Quotes. Accessed January 29, 2024. https://www.azquotes.com/author/18339-Walter_E_Williams.

Banks, Nina. *Democracy, Race, and Justice: The Speeches and Writings of Sadie T. M. Alexander*. Princeton, NJ: Yale University Press, 2021.

Bhutta, Neil, Andrew C. Chang, Lisa J. Dettling, and Joanne W. Hsu. "Disparities in Wealth by Race and Ethnicity in the 2019 Survey of Consumer Finances." *FEDS Notes*, Board of Governors of the Federal Reserve System, September 28, 2020. https://doi.org/10.17016/2380-7172.2797.

Bloom, David E., David Canning, Rainer Kotschy, Klaus Prettner, and Johannes Schunemann. "Health and Economic Growth: Reconciling the Micro and Macro Evidence." Working paper 26003, National Bureau of Economic Research, June 2019, revised June 2022.

Borrelli, Lena. "What Is the Affordable Care Act (Obamacare)?" *Forbes*, last modified February 15, 2024. https://www.forbes.com/advisor/health-insurance/what-is-obamacare/.

Boston Institute of Analytics. "The Future of AI: How Artificial Intelligence Will Change the World." Boston Institute of Analytics, March 28, 2024. https://bostoninstituteofanalytics.org/blog/the-future-of-ai-how-artificial-intelligence-will-change-the-world/.

Britannica. "Arab Spring." Last modified July 13, 2024. https://www.britannica.com/event/Arab-Spring.

Brown, Anna. *More Childless U.S. Adults Now Say They Don't Plan to Ever Have Kids*. Washington, DC: Pew Research Center, November 19, 2021.

Brown, Elizabeth, and Austin Nicholls. *Self-Employment, Family-Business Ownership, and Economic Mobility*. Urban Institute, May 2014.

Burke, Colin B. *American Collegiate Populations: A Test of the Traditional View*. New York: New York University Press, 1982.

Carlson, Scott. "Spending Shifts as Colleges Compete on Students' Comfort." *Chronicle of Higher Education* (August 1, 2014): 20–23.

Carpenter, Surekha. "Expanding Credit Access Through Community Development Financial Institutions." Federal Reserve Bank of Richmond, Econ Focus, Fourth Quarter 2022.

Cohen, Tom. "5 Years Later, Here's How the Tea Party Changed Politics." CNN Politics, last modified February 28, 2014. https://www.cnn.com/2014/02/27/politics/tea-party-greatest-hits/index.html.

Congressional Budget Office. *The Budget and Economic Outlook: Fiscal Years 2013 to 2023*. Congressional Budget Office, February 2013. https://www.cbo.gov/sites/default/files/113th-congress-2013–2014 /reports/43907-BudgetOutlook.pdf.

Cornish, Audie, host. *The Assignment with Audie Cornish*. "The Economy's Bad Vibes." CNN, May 30, 2024. Podcast, 23 min. https://www .cnn.com/audio/podcasts/the-assignment/episodes/909eece6-ae4a-11ee- 8467-d3288baf1c6f.

Council of Economic Advisors. "The Economics of Administration Action on Student Debt." Council of Economic Advisors, April 8, 2024. https://www.whitehouse.gov/cea/written-materials/2024/04/08/the- economics-of-administration-action-on-student-debt/.

Creamer, John, Emily A. Shrider, Kalee Burns, and Frances Chen, *Poverty in the United States: 2021*, United States Census Bureau, September 2022, https://cps.ipums.org/cps/resources/poverty /PovReport21.pdf.

Darity, William Jr., Darrick Hamilton, Mark Paul et al. *What We Get Wrong About Closing the Racial Wealth Gap*. Durham, NC: Samuel DuBois Cook Center on Social Equity, April 2018.

Derenoncourt, Ellora, Chi Hyun Kim, Moritz Kuhn, and Moritz Schular- ick. "Wealth of Two Nations: The U.S. Racial Wealth Gap, 1860–2020." *Quarterly Journal of Economics* 139, no. 2 (May 2024): 693–750. https://doi.org/10.1093/qje/qjad044.

Dharmasankar, Sharada, and Bhashkar Mazumder. "Have Borrowers Recovered from Foreclosures During the Great Recession?" *Chicago Fed Letter*, no. 370, Federal Reserve Bank of Chicago, 2016.

Dizikes, Peter. "Does Technology Help or Hurt Employment?" *MIT News*, April 1, 2024. https://news.mit.edu/2024/does-technology-help-or-hurt- employment-0401.

Dizikes, Peter. "Most Work Is New Work, Long-Term Study of U.S. Census Data Shows." *MIT News*, April 1, 2024. https://news.mit.edu/2024/most- work-is-new-work-us-census-data-shows-0401.

Dube, Arindrajit, and Ethan Kaplan. "Occupy Wall Street and the Political Economy of Inequality." *Economist's Voice* 3, no. 9, March 2012.

Eastland-Underwood, Jessica. "What Was the Original Intent? The Tea Party Movement, the Founding Fathers, and the American Welfare State." *Journal of Political Ideologies* 28, no. 2 (2023): 219–37. https:// doi.org/10.1080/13569317.2021.1956758.

Farrow, Kenyan. "Occupy Wall Street's Race Problem." The American Prospect, October 24, 2011. https://prospect.org/civil-rights/occupy-wall-street-s-race-problem/.

Federal Reserve Bank of St. Louis. "Consumer Price Index for All Urban Consumers: Rent of Primary Residence in West." FRED, Federal Reserve Bank of St. Louis. Accessed August 1, 2024. https://fred.stlouisfed.org/graph/?g=G6ea.

Federal Student Aid. "Public Service Loan Forgiveness." Accessed June 12, 2024. https://studentaid.gov/manage-loans/forgiveness-cancellation/public-service.

Federal Student Aid. "6 Things You Should Know About the SAVE Plan." Accessed June 12, 2024. https://studentaid.gov/articles/6-things-to-know-about-save/.

Fiedler, Matthew. "The ACA's Individual Mandate in Retrospect: What Did It Do, and Where Do We Go from Here?" *Health Affairs* 39, no. 3 (2020): 429–35.

Forbes. "The Causes and Costs of Absenteeism in the Workplace." Last updated April 14, 2022. https://www.forbes.com/sites/investopedia/2013/07/10/the-causes-and-costs-of-absenteeism-in-the-workplace.

"Full List of Obamacare Tax Hikes." Accessed January 29, 2024. https://jeffduncan.house.gov/full-list-obamacare-tax-hikes.

Galea, Sandro, and Nason Maani. "The Cost of Preventable Disease in the USA." *Lancet Public Health* 5, no. 10 (October 2020): e513–14. https://doi.org/10.1016/S2468-2667(20)30204-8, PMID: 33007204, PMCID: PMC7524435.

Geismar, Lily. "America Needs a New Approach on Affordable Housing: History Offers a Guide." *Time*, March 25, 2024. https://time.com/6900050/public-housing-biden-plan-history/.

Gitlin, Todd. "The Left Declares Its Independence." *New York Times*, October 8, 2011. https://www.nytimes.com/2011/10/09/opinion/sunday/occupy-wall-street-and-the-tea-party.html.

Goldin, Claudia. "A Brief History of Education in the United States." Working paper, National Bureau of Economic Research, August 1999. http://doi.org/10.3386/h0119.

Goldin, Claudia, and Lawrence F. Katz. "The Shaping of Higher Education: The Formative Years in the United States, 1890 to 1940." *Journal of Economic Perspectives* 13, no. 1 (1999): 37–62.

Gründler, Klaus, and Niklas Potrafke. "Corruption and Economic Growth: New Empirical Evidence." *European Journal of Political Economy* 60 (2019).

Hasell, Joe. "From $1.90 to $2.15 a Day: The Updated International Poverty Line." Our World in Data, last modified October 17, 2022. https://ourworldindata.org/from-1-90-to-2-15-a-day-the-updated-international-poverty-line.

Hasell, Joe, Max Roser, Esteban Ortiz-Ospina, and Pablo Arriagada. "Poverty." Our World in Data, 2022. https://ourworldindata.org /poverty.

Haskins, Ron. "Decisions That Doom the Future." *Washington Post*, March 30, 2012.

Hawkins, Marcus. "The History of the Tea Party from Its Beginning to Now." Thoughtco, last modified October 27, 2019, https://www .thoughtco.com/a-history-of-the-tea-party-movement-3303278.

Hinton, Alaya. "Don't Become a Parent Until You've Hit These Money Milestones." The Balance, October 20, 2021. https://www .thebalancemoney.com/money-milestones-before-having-kids-4144742.

History.com. "G. I. Bill." Last updated May 27, 2010. https://www.history .com/topics/world-war-ii/gi-bill.

Hoover, Gary A. "Elected Versus Appointed School District Officials: Is There a Difference in Student Outcomes?" *Public Finance Review* 36, no. 5 (2008): 635–47.

Hoover, Gary A. "When User Error Calls for a Product Redesign: Poverty in the United States." *Southern Economic Journal* 91, no. 4 (2025): 1208–12. https://doi.org/10.1002/soej.12726.

Hoover, Gary A., and Erik O. Kimbrough. "An Experimental Study of the Impact of Social Comparison on Investment." *Social Science Quarterly* 97, no. 2 (2016): 350–61. https://doi.org/10.1111/ssqu.12228.

Howell, Sabrina T., Theresa Kuchler, David Snitkof, Johannes Stroebel, and Jun Wong. "Lender Automation and Racial Disparities in Credit Access." Working paper 29364, National Bureau of Economic Research, October 2021, revised November 2022.

Ianchovichina, Elena. *Eruptions of Popular Anger: The Economics of the Arab Spring and Its Aftermath*. MENA Development Report. Washington, DC: World Bank, 2018. https://doi.org/10.1596/978-1-4648-1152-4.

Kaplan, David L., and M. Claire Casey. *Occupational Trends in the United States, 1900 to 1950.* Bureau of the Census Working Paper No. 5. Washington, DC: Government Printing Office, 1958.

Katz, Michael B. *The Undeserving Poor: America's Enduring Confrontation with Poverty.* 2nd ed. Oxford: Oxford University Press, 2013.

Keller, Judith. "A Brief History of Housing in the USA." In *The US Housing Crisis: Home and Trust in the Real Estate Economy.* Cham: Springer Nature Switzerland, 2024. https://doi.org/10.1007/978-3-031-57758-1_4.

Kochhar, Rakesh, and Anthony Cilluffo. *Income Inequality in the U.S. Is Rising Most Rapidly Among Asians.* Washington, DC: Pew Research Center, 2018.

Kuznets, Simon. "Economic Growth and Income Inequality." *American Economic Review* 34, no. 1 (1955): 1–28.

Landes, David S. *The Unbound Prometheus.* Cambridge: Cambridge University Press, 1969.

Liesman, Steve. "TARP Executive Compensation Limits Set at $500,000." CNBC, last modified August 5, 2010. https://www.cnbc.com/id/29003965/.

Malik, Adeel, and Bassem Awadallah. "The Economics of the Arab Spring." *World Development* 45 (2013): 296–313.

Martin, Douglas. "James R. Dumpson, a Defender of the Poor, Dies at 103." *New York Times*, November 8, 2021. https://www.nytimes.com/2012/11/09/nyregion/james-r-dumpson-a-defender-of-the-poor-dies-at-103.html.

Maurrasse, David. *Beyond the Campus: How Colleges and Universities Form Partnerships with Their Communities.* New York: Routledge, 2001.

Mazarei, Adnan, and Tokhir Mirzoev. "Four Years After the Spring." *Finance & Development* 52, no. 2 (June 2015).

McGurran, Brianna. "College Tuition Inflation: Compare the Cost of College Over Time." *Forbes*, May 29, 2023. https://www.forbes.com/advisor/student-loans/college-tuition-inflation/.

McNair, Kamaron. "Household Wealth Grew 30% Between 2019 and 2021—Here's Who Gained the Most." MSN, December 9, 2023. https://www.msn.com/en-us/money/markets/household-wealth-grew-30-between-2019-and-2021-heres-who-gained-the-most/ar-AA1lfiV6.

New York Times. "Farm Population Lowest Since 1850's." July 20, 1988. https://www.nytimes.com/1998/07/20/us/farm-population-lowest-since-1850-s.html.

Occupy Wall Street. "Facts About Occupy Wall Street." October 28, 2019.
    http://occupywallst.org/.
O'Connell, Brian. "Taxes and the Affordable Care Act." Investopedia, last
    modified September 6, 2023. https://www.investopedia.com/articles
    /personal-finance/020714/new-taxes-under-affordable-care-act.asp.
O'Mara, Margaret P. "Beyond Town and Gown: University Economic
    Engagement and the Legacy of the Urban Crisis." *Journal of Technol-
    ogy Transfer* 37, no. 2 (April 2012): 234–50.
Palachko, Jacqueline, Sarah M. Wojcik, and Michelle Merlin. "How ZIP
    Codes Determine the Quality of a Child's Education." AP, November 9,
    2019. https://apnews.com/article/1d856cd98d4c491e8443576b3a817740.
Parkin, Michael. *Microeconomics.* 13th ed. Pearson, 2018.
Pew Research Center. *Wealth Gaps Rise to Record Highs Between Whites,
    Blacks, Hispanics.* Washington, DC: Pew Research Center, July 26,
    2011. https://www.pewresearch.org/social-trends/2011/07/26/wealth-
    gaps-rise-to-record-highs-between-whites-blacks-hispanics/.
Price Waterhouse Cooper. *Sizing the Prize: What's the Real Value of AI for
    Your Business and How Can You Capitalise?* London: Price Waterhouse
    Cooper, 2017. https://www.pwc.com/gx/en/issues/analytics/assets/pwc-
    ai-analysis-sizing-the-prize-report.pdf.
Ray, Michael. "Tea Party Movement." *Britannica*, last modified July 27,
    2024. https://www.britannica.com/topic/Tea-Party-movement.
Romero, Christy L. "The Special Master's Determinations for Executive
    Compensation of Companies Receiving Exceptional Assistance Under
    TARP, Special Inspector General for Troubled Asset Relief Program."
    Official memorandum, Office of the Special Inspector General for
    the Troubled Asset Relief Program, January 23, 2012. https://fraser
    .stlouisfed.org/title/special-master-s-determinations-executive-
    compensation-companies-receiving-exceptional-assistance-tarp-5101.
Sainato, Michael. "'I Live on the Street Now': How Americans Fall into
    Medical Bankruptcy." *The Guardian*, November 14, 2019. https://
    www.theguardian.com/us-news/2019/nov/14/health-insurance-
    medical-bankruptcy-debt.
Schaeffer, Katherine. "Key Facts About Housing Affordability in the U.S."
    Pew Research Center, March 23, 2022. https://www.pewresearch.org/short-
    reads/2022/03/23/key-facts-about-housing-affordability-in-the-u-s/.
Shah, Simone. "The Writers' Strike Is Taking a Stand on AI." *Time*, last
    modified May 4, 2023. https://time.com/6277158/writers-strike-ai-
    wga-screenwriting/.

Shaw, Hannah, and Chad Stone. *Tax Data Show Richest 1 Percent Took a Hit in 2008, but Income Remained Highly Concentrated at the Top.* Center on Budget and Policy Priorities, last updated May 25, 2011. https://www.cbpp.org/research/tax-data-show-richest-1-percent-took-a-hit-in-2008-but-income-remained-highly-concentrated.

Sly, Liz. "The Unfinished Business of the Arab Spring." *Washington Post,* January 24, 2021. https://www.washingtonpost.com/world/interactive /2021/arab-spring-10-year-anniversary-lost-decade/.

Thelin, John, and Marybeth Gasman. "The History of Student Affairs at Colleges and Universities." In *Student Affairs: A Handbook for the Professions,* edited by John Schuh, Susan Jones, and Shaun R. Harper. San Francisco: Jossey-Bass, 2011.

Tough, Paul. "Americans Are Losing Faith in the Value of College: Whose Fault Is That?" *New York Times Magazine,* September 5, 2023. https:// www.nytimes.com/2023/09/05/magazine/college-worth-price.html.

Tuong, Vivian. "6 Incredible Businesses That Started in a Garage." American Express, last updated August 14, 2023. https://www.americanexpress .com/en-us/business/trends-and-insights/articles/6-incredible-companies-that-started-in-a-garage/.

United States Census Bureau. "Historical Income Tables: Households." Accessed August 1, 2024. https://www.census.gov/data/tables /time-series/demo/income-poverty/historical-income-households .html.

United States Census Bureau. *How the Census Bureau Measures Poverty.* Washington, DC: United States Census Bureau, 2021.

United States Census Bureau. *Poverty: The History of a Measure.* Washington, DC: United States Census Bureau, January 2014.

U.S. Bureau of Labor Statistics. "Establishment Age and Survival Data." Accessed November 3, 2023. https://www.bls.gov/bdm/bdmage.htm.

U.S. Citizenship and Immigration Services. "Naturalization Through Military Service." Accessed December 1, 2023. https://www.uscis.gov /military/naturalization-through-military-service.

U.S. Department of Health and Human Services. "About the ACA." Last modified March 17, 2022. https://www.hhs.gov/healthcare/about-the -aca/index.html.

U.S. Department of the Treasury. "About TARP." Accessed January 5, 2024. https://home.treasury.gosv/data/troubled-assets-relief-program /about-tarp.

U.S. Department of Veterans Affairs. "About GI Bill Benefits." Accessed December 1, 2023. https://www.va.gov/education/about-gi-bill-benefits/.

U.S. Small Business Administration. *2020 Small Business Profile.* Office of Advocacy, U.S. Small Business Administration. June 2020. https://advocacy.sba.gov/wp-content/uploads/2020/06/2020-Small-Business-Economic-Profile-US.pdf.

Voices of Welfare. "Truth #5: There Are Many Reasons Women Have Children; Increased Benefits Isn't One of Them." Voices of Welfare. Accessed November 11, 2023. https://blogs.elon.edu/voicesofwelfare/truth-5-there-are-many-reasons-women-have-children-increased-benefits-isnt-one-of-them/.

The Week. "Occupy Wall Street: A Protest Timeline." Last updated November 21, 2011. https://web.archive.org/web/20140209113047/http:/theweek.com/article/index/220100/occupy-wall-street-a-protest-timeline.

Wisman, Jon D. "How the Bourgeoisie's Quest for Status Placed Blame for Poverty on the Poor." Working paper, American University Department of Economics, March 2022.

Index

Founded in 1893,
UNIVERSITY OF CALIFORNIA PRESS
publishes bold, progressive books and journals
on topics in the arts, humanities, social sciences,
and natural sciences—with a focus on social
justice issues—that inspire thought and action
among readers worldwide.

The UC PRESS FOUNDATION
raises funds to uphold the press's vital role
as an independent, nonprofit publisher, and
receives philanthropic support from a wide
range of individuals and institutions—and from
committed readers like you. To learn more, visit
ucpress.edu/supportus.

www.ingramcontent.com/pod-product-compliance
Lightning Source LLC
Chambersburg PA
CBHW031533260326
41914CB00032B/1792/J